The Millionaire's Mindset

How to Reprogram Your Brain for Passive Income Success...

Henry Otasowere

The Millionaire's Mindset

©Copyright 2023 Henry Otasowere, "The Millionaire's Mindset: How to Reprogram Your Brain for Passive Income Success"

All rights reserved

No part of this publication may be reproduced, stored in a retrieval system, or transmitted, in any form or by any means, electronic, mechanical, photocopying, recording or otherwise, without the express written permission of the author.

Otimages Publishers
Printed in the United States of America
Available from Amazon.com, Amazon.de and other retail outlets

First Printing Edition, 2023
ISBN: 9798387046902

Dedication

The Dedication of a book is a powerful and emotional statement, as it represents the author's deepest gratitude and appreciation for those who have supported and inspired them on their journey. In the case of "The Millionaire's Mindset: How to Reprogram Your Brain for Passive Income Success," the Dedication is a heartfelt tribute to the people who have helped shape the author's perspective on wealth and success.

The Dedication of the book begins with a simple yet powerful message: "This book is dedicated to those who dare to dream." This statement sets the tone for the entire book, as it highlights the importance of having a vision and a sense of purpose in life. The author recognizes that not everyone has the courage to pursue their dreams, but they believe that with the right mindset and tools, anyone can achieve financial success.

The Dedication then goes on to thank the author's family and friends for their unwavering support and encouragement throughout their journey. The author acknowledges that without the love and guidance of their loved ones, they would not be where they are today. They express deep gratitude for the sacrifices that their family and friends have made to help them achieve their goals.

The Dedication also acknowledges the role of mentors and teachers in the author's life. The author expresses gratitude for the wisdom and guidance of those who have shared their knowledge and experience, helping them to develop the skills and mindset needed to succeed in the world of passive income. They emphasize the importance of seeking out mentorship and guidance from those who have already achieved financial success, as they can provide invaluable insights and advice.

Finally, the Dedication of "The Millionaire's Mindset" ends with a call to action, encouraging readers to pursue their dreams and unlock their full potential. The author emphasizes that anyone can achieve financial success with the right mindset and tools, and they urge readers to take action and start creating the life they deserve.

Overall, the Dedication of "The Millionaire's Mindset" is a powerful tribute to the people who have inspired and supported the author on their journey to success. It highlights the importance of having a vision, seeking guidance from mentors, and taking action to create the life you want. Through this Dedication, the author sets the tone for the entire book, inspiring readers to believe in themselves and their ability to achieve financial success.

CONTENTS

Foreword vii
Acknowledgments viii
Introduction 1
Part 1 2
The Psychology of Millionaire Success 2
    Chapter 1 3
    The Psychology of Millionaire Success 3
The mindset of a millionaire 7
Millionaires are generous 11
    Chapter One 16
    The power of positive thinking 16
The science behind the millionaire mindset 19
The Power of Neuroplasticity 22
The Role of Positive Emotions 27
The Neuroscience of Visualization 32
The power of "mental rehearsal" 36
Part 1 42
    Chapter One 43
    Goal-Setting for Passive Income Success 43
The importance of setting goals 47
How to set effective goals 50
Tips for staying on track 52
Part 1 58
Write Your Part One Title .... Erro! Marcador não definido.
    Chapter One 59
    Write your Chapter One Title .... **Erro! Marcador não definido.**
Part 1 74
Write Your Part One Title .... Erro! Marcador não definido.
    Chapter One 75
    Write your Chapter One Title .... **Erro! Marcador não definido.**
Part 1 96
Write Your Part One Title .... Erro! Marcador não definido.
    Chapter One 97
    Write your Chapter One Title .... **Erro! Marcador não definido.**

Part 1 ....**107**
Write Your Part One Title .... Erro! Marcador não definido.
    Chapter One 108
    Write your Chapter One Title .... **Erro! Marcador não definido.**
Part 1 ....**115**
Write Your Part One Title .... Erro! Marcador não definido.
    Chapter One 116
    Write your Chapter One Title .... **Erro! Marcador não definido.**
Part 1 .... Erro! Marcador não definido.
Write Your Part One Title .... Erro! Marcador não definido.
    Chapter One .... **Erro! Marcador não definido.**
    Write your Chapter One Title .... **Erro! Marcador não definido.**

Foreword

Welcome to "The Millionaire's Mindset: How to Reprogram Your Brain for Passive Income Success." I am thrilled to be writing the foreword for this groundbreaking book that will change the way you think about wealth creation forever.

In today's fast-paced world, everyone dreams of financial freedom and success, but only a select few ever achieve it. So what sets these successful individuals apart? It's their mindset. In this book, you will learn the powerful techniques and strategies that successful people use to reprogram their brains for success, allowing them to create passive income streams that generate wealth while they sleep.

Henry Otasowere has done an incredible job of compiling the latest research, practical exercises, and inspiring success stories to create a comprehensive guide for anyone looking to transform their financial future. By reading this book, you will gain a deep understanding of the psychology behind millionaire success and learn how to adopt the same mindset and habits of successful passive income earners.

Whether you are just starting out on your wealth creation journey or are looking for fresh insights and strategies to take your income to the next level, "The Millionaire's Mindset" has something for everyone. I guarantee that this book will challenge your thinking, expand your mindset, and give you the tools you need to create the financial freedom you've always dreamed of.

So take the first step towards a more abundant life and immerse yourself in the pages of this incredible book. I promise you won't regret it.

Acknowledgments

First and foremost, I want to express my gratitude to the countless millionaire minds who have shared their insights and experiences with me over the years. Your stories have been the inspiration for this book and have helped shape my own understanding of the mindset and habits required for passive income success.

I also want to thank my family and friends for their unwavering support throughout this journey. Your encouragement and love have been the fuel that has kept me going, even when the path ahead seemed daunting.

To my editor and publisher, thank you for believing in the message of this book and for your tireless efforts in helping me bring it to life. Your guidance and expertise have been invaluable, and I am grateful for the opportunity to work with such a talented team.

Finally, I want to thank my readers, both old and new. It is an honor to share my knowledge with you, and I hope that the insights contained within these pages will help you unlock your own millionaire mindset and achieve the passive income success you deserve.

Thank you all from the bottom of my heart.

With gratitude,

Introduction

Welcome to "The Millionaire's Mindset: How to Reprogram Your Brain for Passive Income Success," the ultimate guide to achieving financial freedom and building a successful passive income stream. This book is designed to help you understand the psychology behind millionaire success and learn how to rewire your brain for success.

In today's fast-paced world, achieving financial independence and creating a steady stream of passive income has become increasingly important. However, it's not always easy to achieve. This is where this book comes in. We will delve into the mindset and habits of successful passive income earners, showing you how to adopt them yourself.

Our goal is to help you overcome your limiting beliefs and negative thinking patterns that may be holding you back from achieving financial success. By the end of this book, you will have the knowledge and tools needed to create a solid passive income stream that will continue to grow and generate income for you for years to come.

In the following pages, we will cover topics such as goal-setting, visualization, affirmations, and other proven techniques for rewiring your brain for success. We will provide practical advice, case studies, and real-world examples to help you implement these strategies in your own life.

So, if you're ready to take control of your financial future and start building a successful passive income stream, then join us on this journey and let's reprogram your brain for success!

PART 1
The Psychology of Millionaire Success

Chapter *1*
THE PSYCHOLOGY OF MILLIONAIRE SUCCESS

Welcome to the world of millionaire success! In this chapter, we'll dive deep into the mindset and psychology of successful millionaires, revealing secrets and insights that will help you to adopt the same mindset and habits that have led to their success.

Section 1: The Millionaire Mindset

The first step to achieving millionaire success is to develop the millionaire mindset. This is a way of thinking that is focused on abundance, success, and achievement. Successful millionaires understand that their thoughts and beliefs shape their reality, and they use this knowledge to their advantage. They have learned how to think positively, visualize their goals, and believe in themselves and their abilities. In this section, we'll explore some of the key components of the millionaire mindset and provide you with practical tips and exercises for developing it.

Section 2: The Power of Habits

One of the biggest secrets of successful millionaires is their habits. Successful millionaires have developed habits that are consistent with their goals and visions, and they use these habits to create momentum and achieve success. In this section, we'll explore some of the most powerful habits of successful millionaires, such as goal-setting, time management, and discipline, and provide you with tips for incorporating these habits into your own life.

Section 3: The Importance of Self-Discipline

Self-discipline is another essential component of millionaire success. Successful millionaires understand that achieving success requires hard work, dedication, and perseverance, and they have developed the discipline necessary to stay focused and motivated even when faced with challenges and setbacks. In this section, we'll explore the importance of self-discipline and provide you with practical tips and exercises for developing it.

Section 4: The Role of Failure

Many people believe that successful millionaires are born with a silver spoon in their mouth or that they have never experienced failure. However, this couldn't be further from the truth. Successful millionaires have failed many times, but they have learned how to turn failure into a valuable learning experience. In this section, we'll explore the role of failure in achieving millionaire success and provide you with tips for overcoming failure and using it to your advantage.

In this chapter, we have explored the psychology of millionaire success, revealing insights and secrets that will help you to adopt the same mindset and habits that have led to their success. By developing the millionaire mindset, incorporating powerful habits, developing self-discipline, and learning from failure, you too can achieve millionaire success. In the next chapter, we'll explore goal-setting, visualization, affirmations, and other proven techniques for rewiring your brain for success.

As promised, here are some more secrets of millionaire success that many people may not be aware of.

One of the most important things to understand about millionaires is that they have a different mindset than most people. They view money as a tool to be used for creating more wealth, rather than as an end goal in and of itself. They understand that by investing wisely and making their money work for them, they can create passive income streams that will continue to grow over time.

Another key factor in millionaire success is goal-setting. Millionaires are not content to simply set small, easily achievable goals - they set big, audacious goals that inspire them to work harder and push themselves to new heights. They also understand the importance of visualizing their goals and affirming them to themselves regularly, which helps to keep them focused and motivated.

But perhaps the most important secret of millionaire success is this: they are not afraid to fail. In fact, they understand that failure is an essential part of the learning process, and that without it, they would never have achieved the success they enjoy today. They are willing to take risks and try new things, knowing that failure is just a temporary setback that can be overcome with persistence and determination.

So if you want to achieve millionaire success, you must first adopt the mindset of a millionaire. You must view money as a tool to be used for creating wealth, set big, audacious goals, visualize and affirm them regularly, and be willing to take risks and learn from your failures. By doing these things, you too can create a life of financial freedom and abundance.

Another important psychological aspect of millionaire success is the ability to take calculated risks. Millionaires understand that risk-taking is a necessary part of achieving great success, and they are not afraid to take risks when the potential rewards are high. However, they also approach risk-taking in a calculated way, thoroughly researching and analyzing potential risks before making any decisions.

In addition to these psychological traits, millionaires also possess certain habits and behaviors that contribute to their success. For example, they are often highly disciplined and focused individuals who prioritize their goals and use their time and resources efficiently. They also tend to be lifelong learners, constantly seeking out new knowledge and skills that can help them achieve their goals.

But perhaps one of the biggest secrets of millionaire success is their ability to generate and maintain passive income streams. Unlike traditional income streams, which require constant work and effort to maintain, passive income streams are generated through investments and other sources that require minimal ongoing effort. Millionaires understand the power of passive income and have developed strategies for creating and maintaining these streams, allowing them to continue to generate income even when they are not actively working.

In this chapter, we will explore the psychology, habits, and behaviors of millionaire success in depth, revealing the secrets of these highly successful individuals and providing actionable advice for readers looking to adopt these same strategies in their own lives. By understanding the psychological traits and habits of millionaires and learning to apply these lessons in your own life, you too can develop the mindset and skills necessary for achieving lasting financial success.

The mindset of a millionaire

Welcome to the chapter on "The Mindset of a Millionaire". In this chapter, I will delve into the secrets of the millionaire mindset, including the habits, attitudes, and beliefs that set them apart from the rest of the population.

One of the most significant secrets of millionaires is their mindset of abundance. They believe that there is an unlimited amount of wealth and resources available, and they operate from a place of abundance rather than scarcity. They do not let fear or limiting beliefs hold them back from taking risks and pursuing their dreams.

Another secret of millionaires is that they have a clear vision of what they want to achieve. They set specific and measurable goals for themselves and work tirelessly towards achieving them. They know exactly what they want and they have a plan in place to make it happen.

Millionaires also have a growth mindset, which means they view challenges and failures as opportunities for growth and learning. They are not afraid to make mistakes and learn from them. They constantly seek to improve themselves and their skills.

Another crucial trait of millionaires is their ability to take action. They do not just sit around waiting for things to happen; they take action and make things happen. They are proactive, driven, and persistent in their pursuit of success.

Finally, millionaires understand the power of collaboration and networking. They know that success is not a solo endeavor and they surround themselves with like-minded people who can help them achieve their goals. They are excellent networkers, and they know how to build strong and meaningful relationships with others.

These are just a few of the secrets of the millionaire mindset. By adopting these habits, attitudes, and beliefs, anyone can develop a millionaire mindset and start achieving their own version of success. In the next chapter, we will delve into goal-setting, which is a critical component of the millionaire mindset.

Millionaires prioritize their health and well-being: While it may seem counterintuitive, millionaires know that prioritizing their health is essential for achieving success. They make time for exercise, healthy eating habits, and stress-reducing activities such as meditation or yoga. This allows them to maintain a clear mind and high energy levels, enabling them to make smart decisions and take action towards their goals.

Millionaires focus on creating multiple streams of income: Most millionaires don't rely on a single source of income. Instead, they look for ways to create multiple streams of income, such as investments, rental properties, or a side business. This not only diversifies their income, but also creates a sense of financial security.

Millionaires are lifelong learners: Successful people are always seeking new knowledge and skills to improve their personal and professional lives. Millionaires understand the value of continuous learning and make it a priority to read books, attend seminars, or even hire coaches or mentors.

Millionaires are risk-takers: Building wealth requires taking calculated risks. Millionaires understand that taking risks is necessary for achieving success and are willing to take chances on new business ventures, investments, or other opportunities that have the potential for high returns.

Millionaires are disciplined with their money: While millionaires may have a reputation for spending lavishly, the truth is that most are extremely disciplined with their money. They set strict budgets, live below their means, and avoid frivolous spending. This allows them to save and invest more of their money, leading to greater wealth over time.

They focus on their strengths: Successful millionaires understand the importance of focusing on their strengths rather than trying to improve their weaknesses. By focusing on what they're good at, they're able to excel in their field and become experts in their industry.

They're not afraid to take risks: Millionaires know that taking calculated risks is a necessary part of achieving success. They're willing to step out of their comfort zone and try new things, even if it means risking failure.

They prioritize self-improvement: Millionaires understand that personal growth is essential for success. They're always looking for ways to improve themselves, whether it's through education, networking, or seeking out mentors.

They're persistent: Success rarely comes overnight, and millionaires know this. They understand the importance of persistence and are willing to keep working towards their goals, even in the face of setbacks and obstacles.

They give back: Many successful millionaires are also philanthropists who use their wealth to make a positive impact on the world. They understand the importance of giving back and are dedicated to making a difference in their communities and beyond.

Millionaires are not afraid of taking calculated risks: One of the defining traits of millionaires is their ability to take calculated risks. They understand that there is always some degree of risk involved in any venture, but they are not afraid to take chances when the potential rewards outweigh the risks. They also do their research and make informed decisions before taking any big risks.

Millionaires focus on building multiple streams of income: Millionaires understand the power of diversification and focus on building multiple streams of income. They don't rely on a single source of income and instead invest in different assets such as stocks, real estate, and businesses to create multiple sources of revenue.

Millionaires prioritize their health and well-being: Many people believe that millionaires are workaholics who sacrifice their health and well-being for financial success. However, this is not true for most millionaires. They understand the importance of taking care of their physical and mental health and prioritize activities such as exercise, meditation, and spending time with loved ones.

Millionaires are lifelong learners: Successful millionaires are always learning and growing. They never stop educating themselves and strive to acquire new knowledge and skills throughout their lives. They also surround themselves with like-minded individuals who can help them grow and learn.

Millionaires are generous

Contrary to popular belief, most millionaires are not greedy individuals who only care about themselves. Many millionaires are actually quite generous and use their wealth to give back to their communities and support causes they believe in. They understand that their success is not just about personal wealth, but also about making a positive impact on the world around them.

One of the surprising secrets of millionaires that many people do not know about is that they are incredibly generous. Contrary to popular belief, many millionaires are not solely focused on accumulating wealth for their personal benefit. In fact, they often view their wealth as a tool for creating positive change in the world and helping those around them.

One of the reasons why many millionaires are so generous is that they understand the power of giving. They know that by giving to others, they can create a ripple effect of positive energy that can impact the lives of many people. Whether it is through philanthropy, volunteering, or simply being kind to others, millionaires understand that their actions can have a profound impact on the world.

Another reason why many millionaires are generous is that they understand the importance of building strong relationships. By giving to others, they can build trust and create a sense of reciprocity that can lead to mutually beneficial partnerships and collaborations. In other words, by being generous, millionaires are able to create a network of support that can help them achieve their goals.

Furthermore, many millionaires understand that their wealth comes with a great deal of responsibility. They recognize that they have been given a unique opportunity to make a difference in the world, and they take that responsibility very seriously. By being generous with their time, money, and resources, they are able to make a positive impact on the lives of others and leave a lasting legacy.

The secret to the generosity of many millionaires lies in their understanding of the power of giving, their desire to build strong relationships, and their sense of responsibility to use their wealth to make a positive impact on the world. By adopting a similar mindset, anyone can cultivate a sense of generosity and use their own resources to make a positive impact on the lives of others.

Strategic giving: Millionaires are often very strategic in their giving, looking for opportunities to make a meaningful impact in areas they care about. They may focus on specific causes or issues, or seek out organizations that have a strong track record of making a difference.

Giving as an investment: Many millionaires see their philanthropy as an investment in the future, rather than simply a way to give back. By supporting education, research, or other initiatives, they hope to create a better world for future generations.

Anonymous giving: While some millionaires enjoy public recognition for their philanthropy, many choose to give anonymously. They may not want the attention or publicity that comes with a high-profile donation, or may simply prefer to give without fanfare.

Time and expertise: In addition to financial support, many millionaires also give their time and expertise to support causes they care about. They may serve on boards or advisory committees, mentor young entrepreneurs, or provide pro-bono consulting services to nonprofits.

Community impact: Millionaires who give locally can have a significant impact on their communities, supporting local businesses and creating jobs. They may also support local charities, schools, or cultural institutions, helping to make their communities more vibrant and resilient.

Overall, the generosity of millionaires goes beyond simply writing checks. They often take a thoughtful, strategic approach to their giving, seeking to create lasting change and make a positive impact in the world.

Another secret of millionaires when it comes to generosity is that they don't just give money, but they also give their time and expertise. Many successful entrepreneurs and business people actively mentor and coach others, sharing their knowledge and experiences to help others achieve their own success.

In addition to this, millionaires often give anonymously. They don't seek recognition or praise for their generosity, but instead give quietly and without fanfare. This is because they understand that true generosity is about giving for the sake of giving, not for personal gain or recognition.

Another aspect of millionaire generosity is their focus on giving back to their community. Successful entrepreneurs often have strong ties to their local communities and understand the importance of supporting and investing in them. This can take many forms, from supporting local charities and nonprofits to sponsoring community events and initiatives.

Overall, the generosity of millionaires is a reflection of their abundance mindset. They understand that there is more than enough to go around and that giving can actually bring more abundance into their lives. By giving freely and generously, they create a positive cycle of abundance and prosperity that benefits not only themselves but also those around them.

They are constantly learning: Millionaires understand that knowledge is power, and they are always seeking to expand their understanding of their industries, markets, and the world around them. They read books, attend seminars, and listen to podcasts to stay ahead of the curve.

They are resilient: Millionaires know that failure is a part of the journey to success. They don't give up easily when things get tough, and they are willing to pivot and adjust their strategies as needed to achieve their goals.

They surround themselves with successful people: Millionaires understand the importance of networking and building relationships with like-minded individuals. They seek out mentors and colleagues who can offer guidance and support on their path to success.

They focus on their strengths: Rather than trying to be good at everything, millionaires focus on their areas of expertise and delegate tasks that are outside of their skill set. This allows them to maximize their productivity and efficiency, and ultimately achieve greater success.

They prioritize their health: Millionaires understand that their physical and mental health are critical to their success. They prioritize exercise, healthy eating, and stress-reducing activities such as meditation or yoga to maintain their energy and focus.

Another secret of millionaires is that they understand the value of networking and building relationships. They know that success in any industry is often based on who you know, and they make it a priority to establish and maintain strong connections with others in their field.

One way that millionaires do this is by attending networking events, conferences, and industry gatherings. They understand that these events provide an opportunity to meet new people, learn about the latest trends and innovations, and establish themselves as a thought leader in their industry.

Another way that millionaires build relationships is by seeking out mentors and coaches. They understand that no matter how successful they become, there is always room for growth and improvement. By seeking out the guidance and advice of those who have already achieved what they aspire to, they are able to learn from the successes and failures of others and accelerate their own path to success.

Finally, millionaires also understand the power of giving back to their community. They often use their wealth and influence to support charitable causes and organizations that align with their values and passions. By doing so, they not only make a positive impact on the world around them, but they also enhance their own reputation and build stronger relationships with others who share their commitment to making a difference.

CHAPTER 2

THE POWER OF POSITIVE THINKING

The power of positive thinking is a driving force in the lives of successful millionaires. They understand that a positive attitude can help them overcome obstacles, stay motivated, and achieve their goals. Here are some secrets of millionaires that many people do not know about when it comes to the power of positive thinking:

Millionaires use positive self-talk: They talk to themselves positively and use affirmations to keep their minds focused on their goals. This helps them to stay motivated, optimistic, and resilient in the face of challenges.

Millionaires surround themselves with positivity: They understand that their environment has a significant impact on their mindset, so they surround themselves with positive people, uplifting media, and inspiring messages.

Millionaires practice gratitude: They take time to appreciate what they have, and this helps them maintain a positive outlook on life. Being grateful for their successes and blessings allows them to attract more abundance into their lives.

Millionaires turn failures into opportunities: They do not see failures as setbacks but rather as opportunities to learn and grow. They use positive thinking to reframe their failures and turn them into stepping stones to success.

Millionaires visualize their success: They use the power of visualization to create mental images of the life they want. By focusing on their desired outcomes, they create a positive and optimistic mindset that helps them stay motivated and take action towards their goals.

Millionaires take care of their physical and mental health: They understand that a healthy mind and body are essential for positive thinking. They exercise regularly, eat healthily, and practice mindfulness and meditation to keep their minds and bodies in optimal condition.

The power of positive thinking is a critical component of the millionaire mindset. By using positive self-talk, surrounding themselves with positivity, practicing gratitude, reframing failures, visualizing success, and taking care of their physical and mental health, millionaires are able to maintain an optimistic and resilient mindset that helps them achieve their goals.

Millionaires don't let setbacks bring them down: One of the secrets of millionaire success is their ability to stay positive in the face of setbacks. They see obstacles as opportunities to learn and grow, and they use positive self-talk to motivate themselves to keep going.

Millionaires focus on what they can control: Rather than worrying about things outside of their control, millionaires focus on what they can control and take action towards their goals. They believe that their thoughts and actions can shape their reality and use positive visualization to help them achieve success.

Millionaires surround themselves with positivity: Millionaires understand the impact of the people they surround themselves with on their mindset. They seek out positive, supportive individuals who uplift them and help them stay motivated on their journey towards success.

Millionaires use gratitude to stay positive: Gratitude is a powerful tool for staying positive, and many millionaires incorporate gratitude practices into their daily routine. They take time to appreciate what they have and focus on the positive aspects of their life, which helps them stay motivated and optimistic about the future.

Millionaires believe in abundance: Another secret of millionaire success is their belief in abundance. They see the world as full of opportunities and believe that there is enough success to go around for everyone. This mindset helps them stay positive and motivated, even in challenging times.

Millionaires understand that thoughts have energy and that positive thoughts attract positive outcomes. They actively work to cultivate a positive mindset by practicing gratitude, visualizing success, and affirming positive beliefs.

Positive thinking doesn't mean ignoring reality or avoiding problems. Rather, it's about approaching challenges with a solution-oriented mindset and seeing opportunities where others see obstacles.

Millionaires also recognize the importance of surrounding themselves with positive people and influences. They seek out mentors, coaches, and like-minded individuals who can offer support, encouragement, and inspiration.

They also understand the impact of negative self-talk and work to replace negative thoughts and beliefs with positive ones. This may involve challenging limiting beliefs, reframing negative experiences, and practicing self-compassion.

Additionally, many millionaires use techniques like meditation, mindfulness, and visualization to quiet their minds, focus their thoughts, and cultivate a sense of inner peace and calm.

Finally, millionaires understand that positive thinking is an ongoing practice, not a one-time event. They make it a daily habit to focus on the positive, stay solution-focused, and cultivate a sense of optimism and possibility. By doing so, they are able to create the kind of mindset that supports success and abundance in all areas of their lives.

The science behind the millionaire mindset

The psychology behind success has always been a topic of interest, and when it comes to the millionaire mindset, science has a lot to say. In this chapter, we will delve deeper into the science behind the millionaire mindset and discover the secrets that many people do not know about.

The Science of Habits

Habits are the building blocks of success, and science has shown that they can be cultivated and strengthened. Millionaires have mastered the art of creating and sticking to positive habits that bring them closer to their goals. In this section, we will explore the science behind habit formation and how it relates to the millionaire mindset.

Habits are the building blocks of success, and millionaires understand this better than most people. The right habits can make or break your journey to financial independence, and understanding how to develop and sustain positive habits is a key component of the millionaire mindset. In this chapter, we will explore the science behind habits, and how millionaires use this knowledge to build the right habits to achieve their goals.

Body:

Section 1: The Science of Habits

- Understanding the Habit Loop: Cue, Routine, Reward
- The Role of the Basal Ganglia in Habit Formation
- The Science of Habit Change: Neuroplasticity and the Power of Repetition

Section 2: Habits of Successful Millionaires

- The Power of Daily Rituals: Examples from Successful Millionaires
- The Habits that Set Millionaires Apart: Consistency, Focus, and Discipline
- Habits that Lead to Financial Success: Goal Setting, Planning, and Execution

Section 3: Building and Sustaining Positive Habits

- Creating Keystone Habits: The Habits that Make Everything Else Easier
- Setting SMART Habits: Specific, Measurable, Achievable, Relevant, and Time-Bound

- The Power of Accountability: Using Social Support to Develop Positive Habits

The science of habits is a powerful tool for anyone looking to achieve financial success. Millionaires understand that habits are the foundation of success, and they use this knowledge to build and sustain the habits necessary to achieve their goals. By understanding the science behind habits, and adopting the habits of successful millionaires, anyone can develop the right habits to achieve financial independence. It takes time and effort to build positive habits, but with persistence and discipline, anyone can develop the millionaire mindset.

Millionaires understand the power of habits: Successful millionaires understand that their daily habits determine their success. They have built habits that support their goals and help them achieve success.

Millionaires develop good habits early on: Millionaires start building good habits early in life. They understand that habits take time to form and become ingrained, so they start early to build good habits that will serve them throughout their lives.

Millionaires are persistent: Developing new habits can be challenging, and it takes persistence to make them stick. Millionaires are persistent in their efforts to build new habits, even when they encounter setbacks or challenges.

Millionaires track their habits: Successful millionaires track their habits and progress to ensure they are staying on track with their goals. This helps them to identify any areas where they need to improve and make adjustments as needed.

Millionaires use the power of routines: Successful millionaires use routines to create structure and consistency in their daily lives. They understand that routines help to eliminate decision fatigue and free up mental energy to focus on more important tasks.

Millionaires focus on one habit at a time: Trying to change too many habits at once can be overwhelming and lead to failure. Millionaires focus on one habit at a time, mastering it before moving on to the next one.

Millionaires have a growth mindset: Successful millionaires have a growth mindset, which means they believe that they can learn and grow throughout their lives. This mindset helps them to be open to new ideas and to embrace change, which is essential for developing new habits.

The Power of Neuroplasticity

Neuroplasticity is the brain's ability to change and reorganize itself throughout life. The millionaire mindset relies heavily on the brain's ability to adapt to new challenges and learn from experience. In this section, we will explore the science behind neuroplasticity and how it can be harnessed to cultivate the millionaire mindset.

The brain is the most complex organ in the human body and it is capable of amazing things. One of the most intriguing aspects of the brain is its ability to change and adapt to new circumstances, a phenomenon known as neuroplasticity. This chapter will explore how neuroplasticity can be harnessed to help develop the mindset of a millionaire.

Secrets of Millionaires:

Many people assume that successful millionaires are born with an innate talent or ability that allows them to accumulate wealth. However, research has shown that the brains of successful individuals are wired differently. In fact, the brains of self-made millionaires are capable of rewiring themselves to create new neural pathways and develop new skills and habits.

One of the secrets of millionaires is that they understand the power of neuroplasticity and actively work to develop their brains in a way that supports their goals. They know that by changing their thought patterns, they can change their behavior, which in turn can lead to greater success.

Harnessing Neuroplasticity:

Neuroplasticity is a powerful tool that can be harnessed to help individuals achieve their goals. Here are some ways to use neuroplasticity to develop a millionaire mindset:

Focus on Growth Mindset: Millionaires understand that their success is not fixed, but rather, it is a result of their growth mindset. They focus on developing their abilities and continually seek new challenges. By doing so, they are able to develop new neural pathways that support their growth and success.

Create Positive Habits: Habits are powerful because they are ingrained in the neural pathways of the brain. To develop a millionaire mindset, it is important to create positive habits that support success. This could be something as simple as waking up early every day or meditating for 10 minutes each morning.

Challenge Your Brain: One of the best ways to develop neuroplasticity is to challenge your brain with new and complex tasks. This could be learning a new language or taking up a new hobby. By doing so, you are creating new neural pathways and strengthening your brain's ability to adapt to new circumstances.

Visualize Success: Visualization is a powerful tool that can help rewire the brain for success. Millionaires use visualization techniques to imagine themselves achieving their goals. By doing so, they are creating new neural pathways that support their success.

Neuroplasticity is a powerful tool that can be used to develop the mindset of a millionaire. By focusing on growth mindset, creating positive habits, challenging the brain, and visualizing success, individuals can harness the power of neuroplasticity to achieve their goals. By understanding the science behind neuroplasticity, anyone can develop the mindset of a millionaire and achieve success.

They believe that change is possible: Millionaires understand that the brain is capable of change and that they have the power to rewire it to achieve their goals. They believe that they can learn and improve continuously throughout their lives, and they take action to make it happen.

They prioritize learning: Successful millionaires are lifelong learners. They are always seeking new information and skills to improve themselves and their businesses. They invest in personal development, attend workshops, and read books to enhance their knowledge and grow their businesses.

They practice visualization and affirmations: Millionaires use the power of visualization and positive affirmations to program their minds for success. They create mental pictures of their goals and visualize themselves achieving them. They also repeat positive affirmations to themselves regularly to build confidence and reinforce positive beliefs.

They challenge themselves: Millionaires understand that the brain grows when it is challenged. They intentionally seek out challenges and set ambitious goals that push them out of their comfort zones. They know that by pushing themselves to their limits, they will grow and improve.

They use the power of positive emotions: Millionaires know that positive emotions, such as joy, gratitude, and love, can have a powerful impact on the brain. They intentionally seek out positive experiences and emotions to build neural pathways associated with happiness and success. They also practice gratitude regularly to cultivate a positive mindset.

By understanding and applying the principles of neuroplasticity, millionaires can rewire their brains to achieve success and create the life they desire.

Here are some additional points to expand on the topic of "The Power of Neuroplasticity" and secrets of millionaires that many people do not know about:

Successful millionaires recognize the power of neuroplasticity and actively seek ways to harness it to their advantage. They understand that the brain is not a static organ and that it is capable of changing and adapting throughout life. This means that they can consciously train their brains to think and behave in ways that support their success.

One of the ways millionaires use neuroplasticity to their advantage is by adopting a growth mindset. They understand that their abilities and talents can be developed through hard work and dedication, and they believe that their potential is not fixed. This helps them to embrace challenges and learn from their mistakes, rather than being discouraged by setbacks.

Another way that millionaires use neuroplasticity is by practicing visualization and mental rehearsal. By visualizing themselves achieving their goals and imagining the steps they need to take to get there, they are strengthening the neural pathways in their brains that support those behaviors. This makes it easier for them to take action towards their goals and stay focused on their vision.

Millionaires also understand the importance of rest and relaxation for brain health and neuroplasticity. They recognize that a tired or stressed brain is less effective at learning and adapting, so they prioritize activities like meditation, exercise, and quality sleep to keep their brains in peak condition.

Finally, millionaires know that habits are a key component of neuroplasticity. By adopting positive habits and routines, they are building new neural pathways in their brains that support their success. This might include habits like regular exercise, healthy eating, journaling, or setting daily goals. By consistently practicing these habits, millionaires are rewiring their brains for success and creating a strong foundation for their achievements.

One secret that many people may not know about the power of neuroplasticity is that it's never too late to rewire your brain. Some may believe that the brain is hardwired and that you're stuck with certain habits and patterns for life. However, studies have shown that the brain has the ability to change and adapt, even in later stages of life.

Another secret is that intentional repetition is key to creating new neural pathways. Just like practicing a new skill or habit, consistently repeating positive affirmations or visualization exercises can strengthen the neural connections in your brain and help solidify the new patterns.

Lastly, it's important to challenge your brain with new experiences and learning opportunities. This can range from trying a new hobby to learning a new language or skill. By constantly stimulating your brain, you can encourage growth and development, which can contribute to the success of your millionaire mindset.

The Role of Positive Emotions

Positive emotions have been linked to success in numerous studies. Science has shown that positive emotions can boost creativity, productivity, and overall well-being. In this section, we will explore the science behind positive emotions and how they can be cultivated to create a more successful mindset.

Positive emotions play a crucial role in the mindset of millionaires. Many people believe that wealth and success bring happiness, but the opposite is often true. Millionaires understand that happiness and positive emotions are the key to success and abundance.

One secret that many millionaires know is the power of gratitude. Being grateful for what you have, no matter how small, can shift your mindset to abundance and attract more positivity into your life. Gratitude is a powerful emotion that can help you focus on the present moment and appreciate the things you have in your life. This positivity can attract more abundance and success.

Another secret of millionaires is the power of joy. When you experience joy, you are in a state of flow, and you attract more positive experiences into your life. Millionaires understand that joy is not just a fleeting emotion but a state of being that can be cultivated through intentional practices like meditation, exercise, and spending time with loved ones.

Many millionaires know the importance of cultivating positive emotions like compassion and kindness. When you show kindness to others, you create a ripple effect of positivity that can impact your life and the lives of those around you. This positive energy can attract more abundance and success into your life.

In this chapter, we will explore the science behind positive emotions and how millionaires use them to create abundance and success in their lives. We will discuss practical tips and exercises for cultivating positive emotions and shifting your mindset to one of abundance and joy.

Millionaires tend to have a positive attitude towards life, and they cultivate positive emotions like gratitude, joy, and love. These emotions help them stay motivated, energized, and focused on their goals. Research has shown that positive emotions can improve our physical and mental health, enhance our creativity and problem-solving skills, and increase our resilience in the face of adversity.

One of the secrets of millionaires is that they practice visualization and positive self-talk to create positive emotions. They use their imagination to create mental images of their desired outcome, and they use affirmations and positive statements to reinforce their beliefs and expectations. This technique can help them build confidence, reduce stress, and stay optimistic about the future.

Another secret of millionaires is that they surround themselves with positive people and avoid negative influences. They understand that emotions are contagious, and they want to be around people who uplift and inspire them. They also know how to manage their emotions and avoid getting caught up in negative thought patterns or limiting beliefs.

In addition, millionaires often practice mindfulness and meditation to cultivate positive emotions. They learn to focus their attention on the present moment and let go of negative thoughts or distractions. This technique can help them reduce stress, improve their mood, and increase their overall well-being. Research has also shown that meditation can increase the size and connectivity of brain regions associated with positive emotions, empathy, and compassion.

Finally, millionaires often use humor and playfulness to create positive emotions. They know how to lighten up and have fun, even in stressful situations. They understand that laughter and joy can boost their creativity, improve their relationships, and enhance their overall quality of life. By incorporating humor and playfulness into their daily routine, they can stay motivated, happy, and successful over the long-term.

Embrace Gratitude: Many millionaires attribute their success to practicing gratitude. Gratitude can help shift your focus from what you lack to what you have, which can help cultivate a more positive mindset.

The Importance of Positive Self-Talk: The way we talk to ourselves can have a significant impact on our emotions and mindset. Millionaires often use positive self-talk to keep themselves motivated and focused on their goals.

The Power of Forgiveness: Holding onto anger and resentment can weigh you down and drain your energy. Millionaires understand the importance of forgiveness and letting go of grudges in order to move forward with a positive mindset.

Practice Mindfulness: Being present in the moment and fully engaged in the task at hand can help you cultivate positive emotions and reduce stress. Millionaires often use mindfulness techniques, such as meditation or deep breathing, to stay focused and calm.

Surround Yourself with Positive People: The people we surround ourselves with can have a significant impact on our emotions and mindset. Millionaires often seek out relationships with positive, supportive individuals who can help lift them up and keep them motivated.

Use Positive Visualization: Visualizing success can help boost your confidence and motivation. Millionaires often use positive visualization techniques to help them stay focused on their goals and achieve success.

Find Joy in the Journey: Millionaires understand that achieving success is not just about reaching the destination, but also about enjoying the journey along the way. Focusing on the positive aspects of your journey can help you stay motivated and cultivate positive emotions.

Many millionaires have mastered the art of gratitude, which is a powerful positive emotion that helps them appreciate the present moment and attract more abundance in their lives. In this chapter, you can explore the benefits of gratitude and provide practical exercises that readers can use to cultivate gratitude daily.

Another positive emotion that successful people often experience is joy. Joy is a state of pure happiness that comes from within, and it's often associated with achieving one's goals, making progress, or experiencing a breakthrough. You can discuss the importance of joy in the context of success and share stories of how joy has played a role in the lives of successful individuals.

Positive emotions such as love and compassion are also critical for developing a millionaire mindset. Many wealthy people are known for their philanthropy and their desire to give back to their communities. By focusing on the needs of others, millionaires are able to build strong relationships, enhance their sense of purpose, and make a meaningful impact in the world. You can discuss the importance of generosity, kindness, and empathy in creating a successful life.

In addition to positive emotions, this chapter can also touch on the importance of emotional intelligence. Many millionaires have developed a keen sense of self-awareness and emotional regulation, which allows them to handle stress, setbacks, and criticism with ease. By learning to manage their emotions effectively, successful people are able to make better decisions, communicate more effectively, and maintain healthy relationships. You can provide tips and strategies for readers to enhance their emotional intelligence and cultivate a more positive mindset.

Millionaires have a positive outlook on life, and they tend to focus on the good things that happen to them. They cultivate gratitude and regularly practice positive emotions like joy, love, and contentment. They know that positive emotions help them maintain a high level of motivation, which is critical for success.

One secret that many people don't know about millionaires is that they intentionally seek out positive experiences. They create positive memories that they can tap into when they need a boost of positive emotions. For example, they might take a vacation to a beautiful destination or attend a concert of their favorite artist. These experiences help them maintain a positive outlook and overcome any setbacks they may encounter.

Another secret is that millionaires surround themselves with positive people who inspire and motivate them. They seek out mentors who have achieved success in their field and surround themselves with colleagues who share their vision and work ethic. They also cultivate positive relationships with family and friends who provide emotional support and encouragement.

Overall, millionaires understand the importance of positive emotions and intentionally cultivate them to maintain a positive mindset and stay motivated.

The Neuroscience of Visualization

Visualization is a powerful tool that many successful people use to achieve their goals. Science has shown that visualization can actually change the structure of the brain and create new neural pathways. In this section, we will explore the science behind visualization and how it can be used to cultivate the millionaire mindset.

Visualization is a powerful tool that can help individuals achieve their goals and improve their overall well-being. It is a technique that many successful people, including millionaires, use to help them achieve their desired outcomes. In this chapter, we will explore the neuroscience behind visualization and how it can be used to achieve success.

One of the secrets of millionaires that many people do not know about is that they use visualization as a tool to help them achieve their goals. Visualization is the process of creating a mental image of a desired outcome or situation. It is a powerful tool that can help individuals achieve their goals by training the brain to focus on positive outcomes.

The science behind visualization is based on the idea of the brain's plasticity or the ability of the brain to change and adapt over time. Visualization is a technique that can help individuals rewire their brains and create new neural pathways. By creating a mental image of a desired outcome, individuals can activate the same neural networks in the brain that would be activated if they were actually experiencing that outcome in real life.

Another secret of millionaires when it comes to visualization is that they use all their senses when they visualize. They create a vivid mental image of their desired outcome, incorporating not just visual but also auditory, tactile, and olfactory senses. By engaging all their senses, individuals can create a more realistic mental image that can help them achieve their goals more effectively.

Moreover, millionaires understand the importance of consistency when it comes to visualization. They make it a daily habit to visualize their desired outcomes, and they do it with focus and intention. This consistency helps to reinforce the neural pathways that are being created and helps to ensure that the desired outcome becomes a reality.

Visualization is a powerful tool that millionaires use to achieve their goals. By understanding the science behind visualization and using it consistently, individuals can rewire their brains and create new neural pathways that can help them achieve success.

Certainly, visualization is a powerful tool used by many successful individuals, including millionaires. One secret that many people do not know is that visualization is not just about picturing yourself achieving your goals. It's also about feeling the emotions that come with achieving those goals. When you can feel the emotions of success, your brain believes that it has already achieved that success and begins working to make it a reality.

Another secret is that visualization is most effective when it's done consistently, and it's not just a one-time event. Successful people often make a habit of visualizing their goals daily, and they use different techniques to enhance the experience, such as adding details to their mental images or creating vision boards.

Visualization works best when it's combined with action. Millionaires don't just visualize their goals; they take massive action towards achieving them. When you combine visualization with action, you send a powerful message to your brain that you are serious about achieving your goals, and it will work to support you in your efforts.

The impact of visualization on the brain: Delve into the science behind how visualization can actually change the structure of the brain, particularly in the areas related to memory, perception, and decision-making. Explain how consistent visualization can create new neural pathways that support the desired outcome, leading to greater success and achievement.

Techniques for effective visualization: Provide specific strategies and exercises that readers can use to improve their visualization skills. This might include guided meditations, visualization scripts, or journal prompts to help readers tap into their creativity and imagination.

Overcoming obstacles to visualization: Acknowledge that visualization can be challenging for some people, particularly those who struggle with anxiety, self-doubt, or negative self-talk. Provide tips for overcoming these obstacles and building a consistent visualization practice, such as starting small, focusing on positive emotions, and using affirmations to support visualization.

The role of visualization in goal-setting: Highlight the ways in which visualization can support goal-setting and achievement, particularly in the context of passive income and financial success. Discuss how visualizing the end result can help clarify and solidify goals, as well as provide motivation and inspiration along the way.

Case studies and success stories: Share examples of successful individuals who have used visualization as part of their millionaire mindset, highlighting the specific strategies and techniques they used to achieve their goals. This can provide inspiration and guidance for readers as they work to develop their own visualization practice.

The power of vivid visualization: Many people think that simply visualizing their goals is enough, but millionaires take it to the next level by creating highly detailed, vivid mental images of their desired outcomes. This helps to activate more areas of the brain and create stronger neural connections.

The role of emotion: Visualization is even more effective when it is accompanied by strong positive emotions. This is because emotions help to activate the brain's reward system, which reinforces the neural pathways associated with the desired outcome.

Visualizing the process, not just the outcome: Successful people know that achieving big goals requires consistent effort and hard work. That's why they visualize not just the end result, but also the process and steps required to get there. This helps to build motivation and a sense of direction.

Combining visualization with action: Visualization alone is not enough to achieve success. Millionaires use visualization as a tool to help them focus their actions and make progress towards their goals. By combining mental imagery with real-world action, they create a powerful feedback loop that reinforces positive behaviors and outcomes.

The power of "mental rehearsal"

One of the most effective visualization techniques used by successful people is "mental rehearsal". This involves mentally rehearsing a specific task or situation, such as giving a presentation or negotiating a deal, in order to prepare the brain and reduce anxiety. This technique has been shown to be highly effective in improving performance and reducing stress.

Mental rehearsal is an incredibly powerful tool that many millionaires use to achieve success in their lives. The principle behind it is simple: you visualize yourself performing the actions necessary to achieve your goals. By mentally rehearsing the steps you need to take, you create a roadmap for success and increase your chances of achieving your desired outcome. This technique is used by athletes, musicians, and successful business people, and it can be applied to any area of life.

One of the secrets of successful millionaires is that they use mental rehearsal to overcome any challenges they may face. They visualize themselves overcoming obstacles and achieving their goals, no matter how difficult they may seem. This helps them to maintain a positive attitude and stay focused on their objectives.

Another secret of millionaires is that they use mental rehearsal to develop a success mindset. By visualizing themselves as successful, they train their minds to think positively and attract success into their lives. This technique can help anyone to develop a success mindset, regardless of their current circumstances.

In conclusion, mental rehearsal is a powerful tool that can help anyone achieve success in their lives. Millionaires use it to overcome challenges, maintain a positive attitude, and develop a success mindset. By visualizing yourself achieving your goals, you create a roadmap for success and increase your chances of achieving your desired outcome.

Let me tell you a secret that many millionaires know and use in their daily lives: mental rehearsal is a powerful tool that can help you achieve your goals and dreams. This technique involves visualizing yourself successfully completing a task or achieving a desired outcome, using all of your senses to create a vivid mental image. By mentally rehearsing your success, you are training your brain to recognize and respond to opportunities that will help you achieve your goals.

One of the keys to using mental rehearsal effectively is to focus on positive outcomes and to be as specific as possible in your visualization. Millionaires know that the more detail you can incorporate into your mental rehearsal, the more powerful it will be. They also know that the more you practice mental rehearsal, the more natural and automatic it will become.

Another secret that many millionaires use when it comes to mental rehearsal is to combine it with action. While mental rehearsal can help you focus your mind and increase your confidence, it is not a substitute for taking action. Millionaires know that taking consistent, purposeful action towards their goals is essential for success, and they use mental rehearsal as a tool to help them stay motivated and focused along the way.

Mental rehearsal is a powerful tool that can help you achieve your goals and dreams. By visualizing yourself successfully completing a task or achieving a desired outcome, you are training your brain to recognize and respond to opportunities that will help you achieve your goals. So start incorporating mental rehearsal into your daily routine and watch as you start to achieve your dreams and reach new heights of success.

The impact of visualization on the brain: Finally, it's important to understand the actual neuroscience behind visualization. When we visualize something, the same areas of the brain are activated as when we actually perform the action. This helps to create new neural pathways and reinforce existing ones, which can lead to lasting changes in behavior and mindset.

By understanding the power of visualization and how it works in the brain, readers can learn how to use this technique to achieve their own goals and create the mindset of a millionaire.

The Impact of Mindfulness

Mindfulness is the practice of being present and fully engaged in the current moment. It has been shown to reduce stress, boost creativity, and improve overall well-being. In this section, we will explore the science behind mindfulness and how it can be used to cultivate the millionaire mindset.

The science behind the millionaire mindset is fascinating and full of secrets that many people do not know about. By understanding the science behind habits. neuroplasticity, positive emotions, visualization, and mindfulness, anyone can cultivate the mindset of a millionaire.

One of the secrets of millionaires that many people don't know about is the power of neuroplasticity. Neuroplasticity refers to the brain's ability to change and adapt based on experiences and behavior. Millionaires understand that by consistently practicing positive habits and thought patterns, they can rewire their brains to think and act in ways that support their success.

Additionally, many millionaires have a deep understanding of the connection between the mind and body. They know that physical health is essential for mental clarity and focus, which are critical components of success. They prioritize exercise, healthy eating, and sufficient sleep to ensure that their bodies are in peak condition to support their success.

Furthermore, successful millionaires often use visualization techniques to help them achieve their goals. They create vivid mental images of themselves achieving their desired outcomes, which helps them stay focused and motivated.

Many millionaires understand the importance of a growth mindset. They see challenges and setbacks as opportunities for learning and growth, rather than as failures. They are willing to take risks and try new things, even if they may initially fail. This attitude allows them to continually improve and achieve greater levels of success.

They understand the power of neuroplasticity: Neuroplasticity refers to the brain's ability to reorganize and adapt to new situations. Millionaires understand that by consistently practicing positive habits and thought patterns, they can actually change the structure and function of their brains to support their success.

They prioritize sleep: Research shows that quality sleep is essential for cognitive function, memory, and decision-making abilities. Many millionaires make it a priority to get adequate sleep each night to ensure they are operating at their best.

They use meditation and mindfulness techniques: Meditation and mindfulness practices have been shown to decrease stress and anxiety while improving focus, attention, and emotional regulation. Many millionaires incorporate these practices into their daily routines to support their mental and emotional well-being.

They cultivate a growth mindset: Millionaires understand that success is not just about talent or luck, but also about persistence and a willingness to learn and grow. They adopt a growth mindset that embraces challenges and sees failures as opportunities for growth.

They prioritize physical activity: Exercise has numerous benefits for both physical and mental health, including reducing stress and improving cognitive function. Many millionaires make time for regular physical activity, whether it's hitting the gym, going for a run.

By understanding the science behind the millionaire mindset and adopting these habits and practices, anyone can begin to rewire their brain for success and achieve their financial goals.

PART 2
Goal-Setting for Passive Income Success

CHAPTER *3*

GOAL-SETTING FOR PASSIVE INCOME SUCCESS

Ah, goal-setting for passive income success, now that's something I could talk about all day! You see, the secret to becoming a millionaire isn't just about working hard and saving money, it's about having a clear vision and setting goals to achieve that vision. One of the most powerful secrets of millionaires is their ability to set goals that align with their vision and work towards them with laser-like focus.

But here's the thing, setting goals isn't just about writing them down and hoping for the best. It's about setting smart, achievable goals that are specific, measurable, attainable, relevant, and time-bound. By setting these kinds of goals, you create a roadmap for success and give yourself a clear target to aim for.

Another secret of millionaires is their ability to break down big, audacious goals into smaller, more manageable ones. This allows them to take action every day and build momentum towards their end goal. They understand that success is built one step at a time and that every small action they take brings them closer to their ultimate vision.

Millionaires understand the importance of accountability when it comes to achieving their goals. They surround themselves with people who support and challenge them, whether it's a mentor, a coach, or a mastermind group. These people hold them accountable to their goals and keep them focused and on track.

In summary, the secrets of millionaires when it comes to goal-setting for passive income success are:

1. Setting smart, achievable goals that align with their vision

2. Breaking down big goals into smaller, more manageable ones

3. Building momentum through consistent action

4. Surrounding themselves with a support system to hold them accountable.

Now, go out there and start setting some goals for your own passive income success!

Millionaires prioritize their time: They understand that time is a precious commodity and make sure to use it effectively. They prioritize their time by focusing on what matters most, setting clear goals, and eliminating distractions.

Millionaires take calculated risks: While it's important to manage risks, millionaires are not afraid to take calculated risks. They understand that every investment has an element of risk and work to minimize it through research and analysis.

Millionaires have multiple streams of income: Most millionaires have multiple streams of income. This helps to diversify their income and reduce their dependence on any single source of income.

Millionaires are lifelong learners: They invest in their education and personal development. They understand that continuous learning is essential to success and growth.

Millionaires have a strong work ethic: Millionaires understand that success doesn't come easy. They are willing to work hard, put in long hours, and make sacrifices to achieve their goals.

Millionaires focus on creating value: Successful millionaires focus on creating value for others. They understand that by providing value to others, they can build strong relationships and generate more business.

Millionaires surround themselves with successful people: They understand the importance of surrounding themselves with successful people who can offer support, guidance, and inspiration.

And let me tell you, my friend, there's one secret that most millionaires know but few talk about openly. It's the fact that wealth and success are not just about hard work and intelligence. It's also about mindset and beliefs. You see, many people have negative beliefs and attitudes about money and success that hold them back. Millionaires, on the other hand, have a positive mindset and beliefs that support their success.

They believe that they can create wealth and that they deserve it. They have a "can-do" attitude and focus on solutions rather than problems. So if you want to be a millionaire, you need to start by working on your mindset and beliefs.

You need to identify and eliminate any negative beliefs that are holding you back and replace them with positive beliefs that will support your success. Remember, the mind is a powerful tool, and with the right mindset and beliefs, you can achieve anything you set your mind to.

One key secret that sets millionaires apart is their mindset around money. They view money as a tool to create more value and opportunities, rather than just as something to accumulate. They understand the importance of investing in themselves, their education, and their businesses in order to create passive income streams that generate wealth over time.

Another secret is their focus on creating multiple streams of income. While many people rely on a single source of income, such as a job or a business, millionaires understand that diversification is key to long-term financial success. They create multiple streams of income through investments in stocks, real estate, and other assets, as well as through creating businesses that generate passive income.

Millionaires understand the importance of taking calculated risks. They are not afraid to take chances and try new things, but they do so in a thoughtful and strategic way. They understand that with every risk comes the potential for reward, and they are willing to take those risks in order to create greater opportunities for themselves and their families.

Overall, the secrets of millionaires are not necessarily complicated or mysterious. They simply involve adopting the right mindset, focusing on creating multiple streams of income, and taking calculated risks in order to create long-term financial success.

The importance of setting goals

Setting goals is an important factor for achieving success in any area of life, and it is no different when it comes to building wealth and becoming a millionaire. One secret of millionaires is that they set clear and specific goals for their financial success. They know exactly what they want to achieve and create a plan to make it happen. They also prioritize their goals and work diligently towards achieving them.

Now, let me tell you a secret that many people don't know about. Millionaires understand the power of setting big, audacious goals. They don't limit themselves by setting small or achievable goals. They dream big and set goals that stretch them out of their comfort zone. By doing so, they push themselves to achieve more than they ever thought possible. Millionaires know that setting goals is not just about the destination, it's about the journey. They enjoy the process of working towards their goals and appreciate the lessons and growth that come along the way.

Another secret of millionaires is that they revisit and adjust their goals regularly. They don't set their goals once and forget about them. Instead, they review their progress and make necessary changes to their goals and plans. This allows them to stay on track and make progress towards their ultimate vision of financial success.

Millionaires understand that setting goals is not enough. They take action towards their goals every single day. They don't wait for the perfect moment or for things to be just right. They take consistent and intentional action towards their goals, even when it's hard or uncomfortable. They know that success requires discipline and persistence, and they are willing to put in the work to achieve their dreams.

Ah, I see you're eager to know more about the millionaire mindset! Well, here's a secret that many people don't know: millionaires don't just set any goals, they set SMART goals. What do I mean by SMART? SMART goals are Specific, Measurable, Attainable, Relevant, and Time-bound. This means that each goal they set is clear and specific, can be measured, is actually achievable, relevant to their overall vision, and has a deadline.

Setting SMART goals is a fundamental practice of successful individuals, and it applies not just to finance but to every aspect of life. By setting SMART goals, you increase your chances of achieving them and fulfilling your vision. Additionally, millionaire mindset often involves having multiple streams of income, investing wisely, and making sound financial decisions.

These individuals understand that money is a tool to create more wealth, and they don't let it control their lives. They view it as a means to an end and use it to create more opportunities for themselves and others. They also surround themselves with like-minded individuals who inspire and challenge them to grow, and they constantly seek new knowledge and skills to further their success.

Millionaires focus on creating multiple streams of income: Many millionaires understand that relying on just one source of income is risky. Therefore, they create multiple streams of income through investments, real estate, and other passive income streams.

Millionaires focus on providing value: Successful millionaires understand that the key to wealth creation is providing value to others. They focus on creating products or services that solve problems for their customers, which in turn generates income for themselves.

Millionaires take calculated risks: Many people think that millionaires got lucky or took big risks to get where they are. However, successful millionaires are strategic in their risk-taking, and often do a lot of research and analysis before making a big decision.

Millionaires prioritize saving and investing: While it may seem like millionaires spend a lot of money on luxury goods, many of them prioritize saving and investing a significant portion of their income. This helps them build long-term wealth and financial security.

Millionaires network strategically: Successful millionaires understand the importance of building relationships and networking. However, they don't just attend any event or social gathering - they strategically choose events where they can meet influential people who can help them achieve their goals.

Remember that becoming a millionaire is not just about making money, it's also about developing a millionaire mindset. This means having a positive attitude towards money, believing that you deserve to be wealthy, and having the discipline to follow through on your goals.

Developing a millionaire mindset takes time and effort, but it's a crucial step towards achieving financial success. So, start by changing your thoughts and beliefs around money, and focus on creating value, taking calculated risks, and building relationships with others. With the right mindset and a lot of hard work, you can achieve your financial goals and become a successful millionaire.

How to set effective goals

Setting effective goals is not just about writing them down or having a clear plan. It's about having the right mindset and approach towards them. One secret that many millionaires follow is setting goals that are not only specific, measurable, attainable, relevant, and time-bound, but also ones that are aligned with their core values and purpose. When your goals are in line with your values and purpose, they become more meaningful and motivating, and you are more likely to stick to them even when things get tough.

Another secret is to make sure your goals are challenging enough to stretch you beyond your comfort zone, but not so unrealistic that they become demotivating. It's essential to strike a balance between having a challenging goal that pushes you towards growth and improvement, and one that is still achievable with effort and dedication.

Finally, successful millionaires understand that setting goals is just the first step towards achieving success. They know that it's important to regularly review and adjust their goals as circumstances change, and to celebrate their progress along the way. They also make sure to break down their goals into smaller, more manageable steps that they can take action on every day, building momentum towards their ultimate success.

Millionaires focus on adding value to others: One of the biggest secrets of millionaires is that they focus on adding value to others instead of just trying to make money for themselves. By providing a valuable product or service, they are able to create a loyal customer base and generate wealth over time.

Millionaires are willing to take calculated risks: While many people are afraid of taking risks, millionaires understand that taking calculated risks is necessary to achieve success. They weigh the potential risks and rewards before making a decision, and are not afraid to take action if they believe the potential rewards outweigh the risks.

Millionaires constantly educate themselves: Successful people never stop learning. They read books, attend seminars, and seek out mentors to continue their education and stay up-to-date with the latest industry trends.

Millionaires take action quickly: Successful people understand the value of time and the importance of taking action quickly. They do not procrastinate and instead take immediate action towards their goals.

Millionaires prioritize their health: Many millionaires understand the importance of good health and prioritize their physical and mental well-being. They know that taking care of themselves allows them to perform at their best and achieve their goals more effectively.

Millionaires surround themselves with other successful people: Successful people understand the power of association and surround themselves with other successful, like-minded individuals. This helps them stay motivated and learn from the experiences of others.

Millionaires do not fear failure: Finally, millionaires understand that failure is a necessary part of the path to success. Rather than fearing failure, they embrace it as an opportunity to learn and grow, and use it to fuel their drive towards success.

Tips for staying on track

One of the most important secrets of millionaires that many people do not know about is the power of accountability. Successful individuals understand that they are accountable to themselves and their goals. They hold themselves to high standards and set up systems to help them stay on track. One such system is having an accountability partner or a mastermind group. These are people who share similar goals and can offer support and guidance to each other.

Another secret of millionaires is their willingness to take calculated risks. They understand that to achieve great success, they must be willing to step out of their comfort zone and take risks. They also know that not all risks will pay off, but the lessons learned from failure are invaluable in moving forward.

In addition, successful people know the importance of self-care. They take care of their physical and mental health, which allows them to perform at their best. They prioritize exercise, healthy eating, and getting enough sleep. They also understand the importance of relaxation and rejuvenation, whether that means taking a vacation or simply taking time for themselves each day.

Finally, successful individuals have a growth mindset. They believe that their abilities can be developed through hard work and dedication. They are constantly learning and seeking new knowledge and skills to help them achieve their goals. They also understand that setbacks and failures are opportunities for growth and use them as motivation to keep moving forward.

One thing that many people don't realize is the importance of taking calculated risks. Successful millionaires understand that in order to achieve big results, they must be willing to take calculated risks and step outside of their comfort zone. This means being willing to invest in new ventures, take on new challenges, and make decisions that may not always be popular.

Another secret of millionaires is the value of time management. Successful people know that time is their most precious resource and they must use it wisely in order to achieve their goals. They prioritize their time and focus on activities that will have the biggest impact on their success, while delegating or eliminating tasks that are less important.

Networking is also a crucial component of success. Millionaires understand that building relationships with others is key to opening up new opportunities and expanding their reach. They attend events, join groups, and actively seek out opportunities to connect with other successful people.

Finally, one of the most important secrets of millionaires is the power of perseverance. Successful people understand that setbacks and failures are inevitable, but it is their ability to persevere through these challenges that ultimately sets them apart. They stay focused on their goals, remain persistent, and are not afraid to try new approaches when faced with obstacles.

Of course, my friend. Here's another secret for you: successful millionaires know how to leverage other people's skills and resources to achieve their goals. They understand that they can't do everything alone, so they surround themselves with a team of talented individuals who can help them accomplish their vision. They also know how to delegate tasks effectively, freeing up their own time to focus on high-level strategic thinking and decision-making.

Another thing that sets millionaires apart is their ability to take calculated risks. They don't let fear hold them back from pursuing their goals, but at the same time, they don't jump into ventures blindly. They carefully evaluate the potential risks and rewards before making a decision, and they're not afraid to pivot if something isn't working out. They understand that failure is a natural part of the learning process, and they use setbacks as an opportunity to learn and grow.

Finally, successful millionaires know the power of persistence. They don't give up easily, even in the face of challenges and obstacles. They have a clear vision of what they want to achieve, and they're willing to put in the hard work and dedication required to make it happen. They know that success is not a one-time event, but a journey that requires ongoing effort and commitment.

Here are some more tips on staying on track to achieve your goals from the perspective of a successful millionaire:

Keep a positive attitude: Believe in yourself and your ability to achieve your goals. Stay optimistic and keep a positive attitude even when faced with setbacks or obstacles.

Keep your goals in mind: Keep your goals visible and in mind by writing them down, creating a vision board, or using other visual aids. This will help you stay focused and motivated.

Break your goals down into smaller steps: Break your larger goals down into smaller, more manageable steps. This will help you avoid feeling overwhelmed and will give you a sense of accomplishment as you complete each step.

Take action every day: Take action towards your goals every day, no matter how small the action is. Consistency is key when it comes to achieving success.

Track your progress: Keep track of your progress towards your goals. This will help you see how far you've come and will motivate you to keep going.

Hold yourself accountable: Take responsibility for your own success and hold yourself accountable for achieving your goals. Don't make excuses or blame others for your lack of progress.

Surround yourself with supportive people: Surround yourself with people who believe in you and support your goals. Avoid negative people who may try to discourage you or bring you down.

Remember, achieving success and reaching your goals takes hard work, dedication, and a positive mindset. Stay focused, stay motivated, and stay on track, and you'll be on your way to achieving your dreams.

Of course, here are some additional tips for staying on track towards your goals:

Celebrate small wins: Every step you take towards your goal is progress, so it's important to recognize and celebrate each milestone you achieve. This can help keep you motivated and focused on the end goal.

Surround yourself with supportive people: Your environment and the people around you can have a significant impact on your mindset and motivation. Seek out individuals who support and encourage your goals, and distance yourself from those who don't.

Practice self-discipline: Self-discipline is essential for achieving any goal. This means making choices that align with your goals, even when it's not the easiest or most convenient option. Set boundaries and prioritize your time accordingly.

Visualize your success: Visualization is a powerful tool for maintaining focus and motivation. Imagine yourself achieving your goal and experiencing the emotions that come along with it. This can help keep you on track when you face challenges or setbacks.

Embrace failure as part of the process: Failure is a natural part of the journey towards success. Rather than getting discouraged by setbacks, use them as an opportunity to learn and grow. Reframe failures as learning experiences and keep pushing forward towards your goal.

Remember, achieving your goals takes time and effort, but staying focused and motivated can help you get there faster.

Millionaires focus on creating value for others: One of the secrets of successful millionaires is that they focus on creating value for others. They are constantly looking for ways to solve problems and make people's lives easier.

Millionaires are always learning: Successful millionaires never stop learning. They invest in their own education and personal development, whether it's through reading books, attending seminars or hiring coaches.

Millionaires prioritize their time: Time is one of the most valuable resources that we have, and millionaires know this. They prioritize their time by focusing on the most important tasks first and delegating or outsourcing less important tasks.

Millionaires take calculated risks: Millionaires understand that taking risks is a necessary part of achieving success. However, they don't take reckless risks. Instead, they calculate the potential risks and rewards before making a decision.

Millionaires surround themselves with successful people: Successful millionaires surround themselves with other successful people. They understand the power of networking and building relationships with other like-minded individuals.

Millionaires have a positive mindset: Millionaires have a positive mindset and focus on abundance rather than scarcity. They believe that there is enough success and wealth to go around, and they are grateful for what they have.

Millionaires are persistent: Millionaires understand that success is not achieved overnight. They are persistent and continue to work towards their goals even when faced with obstacles or setbacks.

Millionaires give back: Successful millionaires often give back to their communities and support charitable causes. They understand the importance of making a positive impact on the world.

These are just a few of the secrets of millionaires. By adopting some of these practices into your own life, you may be able to achieve greater success and abundance.

PART 3
Visualizing Success

CHAPTER *4*

VISUALIZING SUCCESS

Visualization is a powerful tool that millionaires use to achieve success in their lives. They know that success starts in the mind and that visualization is a way to create a mental picture of the future they desire. Here are some secrets of millionaires that many people do not know about when it comes to visualizing success:

They use visualization as a daily practice: Millionaires understand that visualization is not a one-time thing. It's something that they do on a daily basis. They take time to imagine themselves living their dream life, and they do it with clarity and detail.

They use positive affirmations: Millionaires also use positive affirmations during visualization. They repeat affirmations that support their visualization and help them stay focused on their goals.

They visualize the process, not just the outcome: Many people focus only on the end result when visualizing success. But millionaires know that success is a journey, and they visualize themselves going through the process of achieving their goals. They see themselves taking action, making progress, and overcoming obstacles.

They involve all their senses: Millionaires use all their senses when visualizing success. They see, hear, feel, and even smell and taste the things they want to achieve. This helps them create a vivid and compelling mental picture of their desired future.

They visualize with emotion: Finally, millionaires visualize with emotion. They feel the excitement, joy, and satisfaction of achieving their goals. This helps them stay motivated and focused on their vision.

Millionaires use visualization as a daily practice, use positive affirmations, visualize the process, involve all their senses, and visualize with emotion. By adopting these habits, anyone can tap into the power of visualization to achieve success in their own lives.

They use visualization as a tool for motivation: Millionaires use visualization to keep themselves motivated and focused on their goals. They imagine themselves achieving their goals and the rewards that come with it. This helps them stay motivated and driven towards their objectives.

They visualize in detail: Successful people don't just visualize the end result; they also visualize the process of getting there. They imagine themselves overcoming challenges and obstacles, and they envision themselves taking the necessary steps to reach their goals.

They make their visualizations a habit: Millionaires make it a daily habit to visualize their goals and success. They set aside time each day to meditate or visualize, and they make it a priority.

They use all their senses: Successful people don't just see their success; they also use their other senses to make their visualizations more powerful. They imagine the sounds, smells, and feelings associated with achieving their goals.

They share their visions: Millionaires often share their vision and goals with others. This helps them stay accountable and also allows others to offer support and encouragement.

They take action: Visualization alone is not enough; millionaires also take action towards their goals. They use their visualizations as a tool for motivation and then take the necessary steps to make their vision a reality.

They stay positive: Successful people maintain a positive mindset, even in the face of setbacks or obstacles. They use visualization to stay focused on their goals and to maintain a positive outlook on life.

Overall, visualization is a powerful tool that can help you achieve your goals and reach your full potential. By adopting the habits and mindset of successful people, you can use visualization to create the life you want and become a millionaire yourself.

Millionaires believe in the power of visualization: Millionaires understand that what they focus on expands and that visualization is a powerful tool for manifesting success. They visualize themselves achieving their goals, and they focus on the positive emotions and feelings associated with that success.

They use affirmations to reinforce their beliefs: Affirmations are powerful statements that reinforce positive beliefs and attitudes. Millionaires use affirmations to remind themselves of their goals, their capabilities, and their commitment to success.

They surround themselves with positive influences: Millionaires know that their environment plays a significant role in their success. They surround themselves with people who inspire and motivate them, and they minimize their exposure to negative influences.

They maintain a growth mindset: Millionaires understand that success requires continuous learning and growth. They remain open to new ideas and perspectives, and they are willing to take risks and try new approaches.

They take inspired action: Visualization and affirmations are important, but they are not enough on their own. Millionaires understand that success requires action, and they take consistent, inspired action toward their goals.

By adopting these practices and making them a part of your daily routine, you can start to unlock the power of visualization and manifest success in your own life. Remember that success is not just about what you do, but also about who you are and how you think. By cultivating a millionaire mindset and staying focused on your goals, you can achieve the success and abundance you desire.

I can tell you that one secret of millionaires that many people do not know about is that they are constantly learning and seeking new knowledge. Successful people understand that they do not know everything and are willing to invest time, effort, and resources into expanding their knowledge and skills.

Millionaires are often voracious readers and are always looking for ways to improve their businesses and personal lives. They attend seminars, workshops, and conferences to gain new insights and network with other successful people.

They also seek out mentors and coaches who can provide guidance and support.

Another secret of millionaires is that they are willing to take calculated risks. They understand that growth and success often require stepping outside of their comfort zone and taking action, even when there is some level of uncertainty involved. However, successful people do not take reckless risks; instead, they carefully evaluate the potential rewards and risks before making a decision.

Finally, millionaires know the value of persistence and perseverance. They understand that success is not achieved overnight and that setbacks and obstacles are a natural part of the process. Instead of giving up, successful people use these challenges as opportunities to learn, grow, and become stronger. They are willing to put in the hard work and effort required to achieve their goals, even when the going gets tough.

By adopting these principles and making them a part of your own life, you too can achieve success and financial freedom.

They visualize their goals as if they have already been achieved: Successful people have a clear vision of what they want and visualize it as if it has already happened. They see themselves living in their dream house, driving their dream car, and enjoying the lifestyle they desire. This helps to reinforce their beliefs and keeps them motivated to take action towards achieving their goals.

They use visualization to overcome obstacles: Millionaires also use visualization to overcome obstacles that may arise on their journey to success. They imagine themselves finding solutions to challenges and visualize themselves succeeding in spite of any setbacks or hurdles.

They practice visualization regularly: Visualization is not a one-time event, it's a habit. Millionaires practice visualization regularly to keep their goals at the forefront of their minds and to reinforce their beliefs. They use visualization as a tool for staying motivated and focused on their goals.

They use all their senses when visualizing: Successful people don't just visualize their goals, they use all their senses to create a vivid and realistic mental image. They hear the sounds, smell the scents, feel the sensations, and taste the flavors of their desired outcome.

They visualize themselves helping others: Finally, millionaires use visualization to not only achieve their own goals but also to help others. They see themselves as successful leaders who make a positive impact on the world around them. By visualizing themselves helping others, they stay motivated to achieve their goals and make a difference in the lives of others.

The role of visualization in achieving success

Visualization is a powerful tool that many successful millionaires use to achieve their goals. It involves creating a mental image of the desired outcome and holding that image in your mind as if it has already happened. Here are some secrets that many people may not know about the role of visualization in achieving success:

1. Visualization is not just about positive thinking.

Many people think that visualization is simply about thinking positively, but it's more than that. Visualization involves creating a vivid mental image of the outcome you want to achieve and imagining every detail of it. This helps to focus your mind and energies on achieving that goal.

2. Visualization helps to reprogram your subconscious mind.

Visualization is a powerful tool that helps to reprogram your subconscious mind. Your subconscious mind is responsible for your beliefs, habits, and behaviors. By visualizing your desired outcome repeatedly, you can reprogram your subconscious mind to believe that you can achieve your goals. This will help to remove any limiting beliefs that may be holding you back.

3. Visualization helps to improve performance.

Many athletes use visualization to improve their performance. They visualize themselves performing at their best and achieving their goals. This helps to improve their confidence, focus, and motivation, which translates into better performance on the field.

4. Visualization helps to attract opportunities.

Visualization is also a powerful tool for attracting opportunities. When you visualize your desired outcome, you are sending a message to the universe that you are ready and open to receive it. This helps to attract opportunities and resources that will help you achieve your goals.

5. Visualization is not a substitute for action.

While visualization is a powerful tool for achieving success, it's not a substitute for action. You still need to take action towards your goals. Visualization helps to focus your mind and energies on achieving your goals, but you still need to put in the work to make them happen.

Visualization is a powerful tool that successful millionaires use to achieve their goals. By creating a vivid mental image of your desired outcome, you can reprogram your subconscious mind, improve your performance, attract opportunities, and ultimately achieve success.

Use all your senses: Successful people use not only their visual sense but also their other senses such as touch, sound, taste, and smell. The more vividly you can imagine your success, the more powerful your visualization will be.

Visualize consistently: Don't just visualize your success once and forget about it. Make it a daily habit to visualize your goals and what success looks like for you.

Focus on the process, not just the outcome: While it's important to visualize achieving your goals, it's equally important to visualize the steps you need to take to get there. By focusing on the process, you'll be more likely to take action and stay motivated.

Use positive affirmations: Affirmations are statements that reinforce positive thoughts and beliefs. Use affirmations that align with your goals and repeat them to yourself during your visualization practice.

Embrace the emotions: When visualizing success, allow yourself to feel the emotions that come with it. Whether it's excitement, joy, or gratitude, these positive emotions can help motivate you to take action and achieve your goals.

Remember, visualization is a powerful tool that can help you achieve success in all areas of your life. By consistently practicing visualization and using these millionaire secrets, you can train your mind to see and attract the success you desire.

Use all your senses when visualizing: Millionaires know that the more senses you involve in your visualization, the more powerful it will be. So when you're visualizing your success, try to not just see it, but also feel it, hear it, smell it, and even taste it if possible.

Visualize the process, not just the outcome: While it's important to visualize the end result you want to achieve, don't forget to also visualize the steps you'll take to get there. This will help you stay motivated and on track as you work towards your goal.

Visualize in detail: The more detailed and specific your visualization is, the more effective it will be. So instead of just picturing yourself in a big house, visualize the color of the walls, the furniture, the artwork on the walls, and even the view out the window.

Visualize consistently: Visualization is a powerful tool, but it's not a one-time thing. Millionaires know that to see real results, you need to visualize consistently and make it a part of your daily routine.

Use visualization to overcome obstacles: When faced with challenges or setbacks, visualization can be a powerful way to stay motivated and focused on your goals. Use it to visualize yourself overcoming obstacles and achieving success, even when things get tough.

By incorporating these visualization secrets into your daily routine, you can tap into the power of your mind to achieve success in all areas of your life.

They visualize consistently: Millionaires understand the power of visualization and make it a regular practice. They take time each day to visualize their goals, dreams, and desires as if they have already achieved them.

They use all their senses: Millionaires don't just visualize in their mind's eye; they engage all their senses in the experience. They feel the emotions, hear the sounds, and even smell and taste the environment they are visualizing.

They visualize in detail: Millionaires don't just see a vague image of their desired outcome. They visualize every detail, from the colors and textures to the people and objects around them. This level of detail helps them to create a more vivid and powerful experience.

They use visualization to overcome challenges: When faced with a difficult situation or obstacle, millionaires use visualization to help them overcome it. They visualize themselves finding a solution and succeeding in the face of adversity.

They use visualization to build confidence: Visualization is a powerful tool for building confidence and self-belief. Millionaires use it to visualize themselves succeeding and achieving their goals, which helps to reinforce their belief in their abilities.

Overall, visualization is a powerful tool that millionaires use to achieve success. By consistently visualizing their goals and desires, using all their senses, and visualizing in detail, they are able to create a powerful experience that helps them stay focused, motivated, and on track towards achieving their goals.

Techniques for effective visualization

One of the most important aspects of visualization is to make it as vivid and realistic as possible. You want to create a mental picture that is so clear and detailed that it feels like you're actually living it. To do this, you should use all of your senses when you visualize. See, hear, feel, smell, and even taste the experience you're imagining.

Another important technique is to focus on the emotions you would feel if you were actually experiencing your desired outcome. For example, if you're visualizing yourself as a successful entrepreneur, focus on the feelings of excitement, confidence, and satisfaction that you would feel in that role. By connecting with these emotions, you can create a strong emotional connection to your goal, which will motivate you to work towards it.

It's also important to visualize yourself as already having achieved your goal. Instead of seeing yourself working towards your goal, see yourself as already having accomplished it. This creates a sense of certainty and inevitability that can help you overcome any doubts or fears you may have.

Finally, it's important to practice visualization regularly. Set aside time each day to visualize your goals and dreams, and make it a regular part of your routine. This will help you stay focused and motivated, and will increase your chances of achieving the success you desire.

As for secrets of millionaires, one thing that many successful people do is to use visualization to create a clear and compelling vision of what they want to achieve. They see themselves as already having achieved their goals, and they use this visualization to stay focused and motivated as they work towards their dreams. By using visualization in this way, they are able to stay committed to their goals and overcome any obstacles that may arise along the way.

Use all your senses: When visualizing your success, it's important to engage all your senses. Imagine what it would look, feel, smell, taste, and sound like to achieve your goals. This makes the experience more real and helps you tap into the emotions and motivation needed to make it a reality.

Make it a habit: Consistency is key when it comes to visualization. Make it a daily habit to take some time to visualize your success. This helps to keep your goals top of mind and reinforces the mental pathways needed to make them a reality.

Be specific: The more specific you can be in your visualizations, the better. Instead of just imagining vague success, imagine specific scenarios that would represent success for you. For example, if your goal is to buy a new house, visualize the exact house you want to buy and what it would look like both inside and outside.

Use visual aids: Visual aids such as vision boards or pictures of your goals can be a powerful tool in effective visualization. These aids help to keep your goals top of mind and reinforce the image of success in your mind.

Believe in yourself: One of the most important aspects of effective visualization is believing in yourself and your ability to achieve your goals. When you truly believe in yourself, you tap into a powerful force that can help you overcome obstacles and achieve your dreams.

By using these techniques and focusing on the power of visualization, millionaires have been able to achieve incredible success in their lives.

How to integrate visualization into your daily routine

Visualization is a powerful tool that can help you achieve your goals and create the life you desire. Here are some secrets of millionaires when it comes to integrating visualization into your daily routine:

Make it a habit: Successful people know that habits are key to achieving success. To make visualization a habit, set aside a specific time each day to practice. Whether it's in the morning, before bed, or during a mid-day break, consistency is key.

Use all your senses: When visualizing, it's important to use all your senses to make the experience as real as possible. This means not only seeing your goals, but also feeling, hearing, and even smelling and tasting them.

Create a detailed mental picture: To make your visualization practice effective, it's important to create a detailed mental picture of what you want to achieve. The more vivid and specific your visualization is, the more powerful it will be.

Be positive: Millionaires understand that positive energy attracts positive results. Focus on positive outcomes and feelings when visualizing, and try to let go of any negative thoughts or doubts.

Use visualization to overcome obstacles: Visualization can also be a powerful tool for overcoming obstacles and challenges. When faced with a difficult situation, visualize yourself successfully navigating through it with ease.

Be grateful: Gratitude is an important part of achieving success, and visualization can be a great way to practice gratitude. As you visualize your goals, take a moment to be grateful for all the things you already have in your life.

Stay flexible: While it's important to have a clear vision of what you want to achieve, it's also important to stay flexible and open to new opportunities and ideas. Use visualization to stay focused on your goals, but be open to new paths that may lead you there.

By integrating visualization into your daily routine and following these tips, you can harness the power of your imagination to achieve the success you desire.

Consistency is key: Successful people don't just visualize once and forget about it. They make it a consistent part of their daily routine. Set aside time each day to visualize your goals and dreams, and stick to it.

Use affirmations: In addition to visualizing, use affirmations to reinforce positive thoughts and beliefs. Create a list of positive affirmations that align with your goals and repeat them to yourself every day.

Use all your senses: Visualization isn't just about seeing things in your mind's eye. Engage all your senses to create a vivid mental picture. Imagine the sounds, smells, and feelings associated with achieving your goals.

Get into a relaxed state: Visualization is most effective when you're in a relaxed and receptive state. Find a quiet place where you won't be interrupted and take a few deep breaths to calm your mind and body.

Believe in yourself: Visualization only works if you truly believe that you can achieve your goals. Focus on building your self-confidence and belief in yourself through positive self-talk, affirmations, and surrounding yourself with supportive people.

Remember, visualization is just one tool in the toolbox of successful people. It's important to pair it with other strategies like goal-setting, action planning, and accountability to achieve the success you desire.

PART 4
The Power of Affirmations

CHAPTER 5
THE POWER OF AFFIRMATIONS

Affirmations are a powerful tool that many millionaires use to achieve success. An affirmation is a positive statement that you repeat to yourself to help change your beliefs and behaviors. By using affirmations, you can shift your mindset from one of negativity and doubt to one of positivity and confidence. Here are some secrets of millionaires when it comes to using affirmations:

Use positive language: Affirmations should be worded in a positive way, focusing on what you want to achieve rather than what you want to avoid. For example, instead of saying "I don't want to be broke," say "I am financially abundant."

Be specific: Make your affirmations specific to your goals. If you want to become a millionaire, your affirmation might be "I am a millionaire and my wealth grows every day."

Believe in what you are saying: Affirmations are most effective when you truly believe in what you are saying. If you have doubts, work on changing your beliefs first.

Repeat your affirmations often: The more you repeat your affirmations, the more they will become ingrained in your subconscious mind. You can repeat them silently to yourself throughout the day, write them down, or record yourself saying them and listen to the recording regularly.

Use present tense: Affirmations should be phrased in the present tense, as if the desired outcome has already happened. This helps to create the feeling of already having achieved your goal.

By using affirmations regularly, you can train your mind to focus on positive outcomes and create the beliefs and behaviors that lead to success.

One important thing to remember is that affirmations should be focused on what you want to achieve, rather than what you want to avoid or eliminate. For example, instead of saying "I don't want to be in debt anymore," rephrase it as "I am financially abundant and free." This helps to keep your mind focused on positive outcomes, rather than dwelling on negative situations.

Another secret of millionaires is to use affirmations in conjunction with visualization. By imagining yourself already having achieved your goals, and repeating affirmations that reinforce those images, you can more effectively train your subconscious mind to attract success and abundance.

It's also important to use affirmations consistently and with conviction. Don't just repeat them mindlessly - feel the power and truth behind each statement. Make them a part of your daily routine, saying them in the morning and before bed, and throughout the day as needed.

Don't be afraid to personalize your affirmations to make them more meaningful to you. Use language that resonates with your values and beliefs, and focus on the areas of your life where you most want to see growth and improvement. With practice and dedication, affirmations can be a powerful tool for achieving your goals and reaching new heights of success.

Affirmations must be in the present tense: One of the secrets of millionaires when it comes to affirmations is that they always state their affirmations in the present tense. They don't say, "I will be rich." Instead, they say, "I am rich." This helps to program their subconscious mind to believe that they already have what they want.

Use positive language: Millionaires know that the language they use is important. They use positive language in their affirmations and avoid negative words like "don't," "can't," or "won't." They focus on what they want to achieve, rather than what they want to avoid.

Repeat affirmations consistently: Consistency is key when it comes to affirmations. Millionaires repeat their affirmations several times a day, every day. This helps to reinforce the positive messages in their minds and reinforces the belief that they can achieve their goals.

Believe in affirmations: One of the secrets of millionaires is that they truly believe in the power of affirmations. They know that affirmations are not just positive statements but a way to change their mindset and reprogram their subconscious mind. They have faith in the process and trust that it will work for them.

Visualize affirmations: Millionaires often visualize their affirmations to make them more powerful. They close their eyes and imagine themselves already having achieved their goals. This visualization reinforces the affirmations and makes them feel more real.

Use affirmations to overcome fear: Millionaires use affirmations to overcome their fears and limiting beliefs. They turn their negative thoughts into positive ones by affirming what they want to achieve. This helps them to move past their fears and take action towards their goals.

Use affirmations to increase motivation: Affirmations can be a powerful tool to increase motivation. Millionaires use affirmations to remind themselves of why they want to achieve their goals and to stay focused on their vision. This helps to increase their motivation and drive to succeed.

Remember, affirmations are not a magic solution, but they can be a powerful tool to change your mindset and achieve your goals. Use them consistently, believe in them, and visualize them to make them even more powerful.

Millionaires focus on creating value: Successful millionaires focus on creating value for others. They aim to solve problems and provide solutions that are in demand in the market. By creating value, they are able to generate income and wealth.

Millionaires invest in themselves

Millionaires invest in their own personal and professional development. They read books, attend seminars and workshops, and seek the guidance of mentors and coaches. They recognize that the more they learn and grow, the more they can achieve.

One of the key secrets of millionaires is that they understand the importance of investing in themselves. They realize that they are their most valuable asset and that their success and wealth ultimately depends on their own personal growth and development.

One way that millionaires invest in themselves is through education. They are constantly seeking out new knowledge and skills to improve themselves and their businesses. They attend seminars, read books, take courses, and hire coaches or mentors to guide them along the way.

In addition to education, millionaires also invest in their health and well-being. They know that their physical and mental health are crucial to their success, so they make sure to take care of themselves through exercise, healthy eating habits, and stress-management techniques.

Another way that millionaires invest in themselves is by surrounding themselves with positive influences. They seek out like-minded individuals who can provide support, guidance, and inspiration. They also avoid negative people and environments that can bring them down and hinder their growth.

Ultimately, the secret to investing in yourself as a millionaire is to make it a lifelong habit. By continuously learning, growing, and taking care of yourself, you can achieve greater success and fulfillment in all areas of your life.

Another secret of millionaires is that they are always looking for ways to improve themselves, whether it's through education, personal development, or acquiring new skills. They understand that the more they invest in themselves, the more they can achieve and the more valuable they become.

One way millionaires invest in themselves is through attending seminars and workshops, reading books, and listening to audio programs. They know that there is always more to learn, and they are constantly seeking out new knowledge and perspectives.

Another way millionaires invest in themselves is by hiring coaches and mentors. They understand that having a mentor can help them navigate challenges and achieve their goals more efficiently. They are willing to invest in the expertise and guidance of someone who has already achieved the success they desire.

Finally, millionaires invest in their health and well-being. They understand that they can't achieve their goals if they are not in good physical and mental shape. They prioritize exercise, healthy eating, and getting enough rest and relaxation. They also make time for activities that bring them joy and fulfillment, such as hobbies and spending time with loved ones.

By investing in themselves, millionaires are able to continually improve and achieve greater levels of success and fulfillment in their lives.

Millionaires live below their means

Many millionaires are frugal and live below their means. They do not spend money on unnecessary expenses and instead focus on investing and saving their money. By living below their means, they are able to accumulate wealth and achieve financial freedom.

Living below your means is a fundamental principle of wealth creation that many people overlook. Millionaires know that in order to accumulate wealth, they must spend less than they earn and save and invest the difference.

One of the secrets of millionaires is that they prioritize their spending. They focus on spending money on things that truly matter to them, and they are willing to forego frivolous purchases in order to achieve their long-term financial goals. They also understand that material possessions do not bring lasting happiness, so they don't feel the need to keep up with the Joneses.

Another secret of millionaires is that they are frugal in some areas so that they can splurge in others. They may drive a modest car and live in a modest home, but they might also enjoy frequent travel or expensive hobbies. They understand that money is a tool to be used to create the life they want, and they make intentional choices about how they use it.

In addition to being mindful of their spending, millionaires are also diligent savers. They prioritize saving and investing a portion of their income, even if it means sacrificing some short-term pleasures. They understand that by saving and investing, they are setting themselves up for long-term financial success.

Finally, millionaires are not afraid to seek out bargains and negotiate for the best deals. They understand the value of their money and are willing to put in the effort to get the most bang for their buck. By living below their means and being intentional with their spending, millionaires are able to build wealth and create a life of financial freedom.

They prioritize saving and investing: Millionaires understand the importance of building wealth through saving and investing. They often live below their means to ensure they have enough money to invest in their future.

They focus on value: Millionaires are often more interested in value than in price. They will spend money on things that provide long-term value, such as education or a quality piece of equipment, rather than just buying something cheap in the moment.

They avoid debt: Millionaires know that debt can be a slippery slope and will do their best to avoid it. They may use credit cards for convenience, but they pay them off in full every month.

They track their spending: Millionaires often track their spending to ensure they are staying within their means. They may use a budgeting app or software to help them stay on top of their finances.

They live modestly: Millionaires often live in modest homes and drive modest cars. They understand that material possessions are not what brings true happiness and fulfillment in life.

By living below their means, millionaires are able to build wealth, maintain financial stability, and enjoy a comfortable lifestyle without overspending.

They understand the difference between wants and needs: Millionaires prioritize their needs over their wants. They understand that buying something that they want may not be the best use of their money if they don't need it.

They don't try to keep up with the Joneses: Millionaires don't feel the need to keep up with their neighbors or friends. They know that just because someone else has something doesn't mean they need it too.

They use coupons and buy in bulk: Millionaires aren't afraid to use coupons or buy in bulk when it makes sense. They know that small savings can add up over time.

They negotiate: Millionaires are often skilled negotiators. They negotiate prices on everything from cars to homes to business deals, which helps them get the best value for their money.

They avoid debt: Millionaires avoid debt whenever possible. They understand that debt can be a trap that keeps them from achieving their financial goals.

They invest in appreciating assets: Millionaires focus on investing in assets that appreciate over time, such as real estate or stocks. This helps them build wealth while also living below their means.

They focus on value, not price: Millionaires focus on getting the best value for their money, not just the lowest price. They understand that a higher quality item may actually save them money in the long run.

Overall, living below their means is one of the keys to financial success for millionaires. By prioritizing their needs over their wants and focusing on value, they're able to build wealth while still enjoying their lives.

Millionaires take calculated risks: Successful millionaires take calculated risks in order to achieve their goals. They do their research and analyze potential outcomes before making a decision. By taking calculated risks, they are able to seize opportunities and create wealth.

Millionaires focus on long-term goals: Millionaires have a long-term focus when it comes to their financial goals. They understand that achieving financial success takes time and effort, and they are willing to make sacrifices in the short-term in order to achieve their long-term goals.

Millionaires have a positive attitude: Successful millionaires have a positive attitude towards life and their goals. They believe that they can achieve their dreams and are willing to work hard to make them a reality. Their positive attitude helps them stay motivated and focused on their goals.

Millionaires network with successful people: Successful millionaires surround themselves with other successful people. They attend networking events, join mastermind groups, and seek out mentors who can help them achieve their goals. By networking with successful people, they are able to learn from their experiences and accelerate their own success.

Millionaires are disciplined

Successful millionaires are disciplined in their daily routines and habits. They set goals, create plans, and follow through on their commitments. Their discipline helps them stay focused and achieve their goals.

One of the biggest secrets of millionaires that many people don't know about is their exceptional level of discipline. Millionaires understand that success is a marathon, not a sprint, and they consistently practice discipline in their daily lives to stay focused on their goals.

One area where millionaires show their discipline is in their spending habits. They avoid impulsive purchases and make thoughtful, strategic decisions about where to spend their money. They also make a habit of saving a portion of their income, even when times are good, so that they have a financial cushion in case of emergencies or downturns in the economy.

Another area where millionaires demonstrate discipline is in their daily routines. They understand that success is built on consistent, focused effort over time, so they make sure to prioritize the most important tasks and activities in their day. They also make a habit of setting clear goals and holding themselves accountable for achieving those goals.

Finally, millionaires understand the importance of investing in their own personal development. They recognize that there is always more to learn and ways to improve, and they consistently seek out opportunities to grow their knowledge and skills.

The secret to millionaire-level success is a combination of financial discipline, focused daily routines, and ongoing personal development. By adopting these habits and approaches, anyone can set themselves up for long-term success and achieve their goals.

They prioritize their time: Millionaires are disciplined about how they use their time. They know that time is a valuable resource, and they prioritize tasks that are essential to their success. They plan their day and stick to a schedule to ensure they are making progress towards their goals.

They have a strong work ethic: Millionaires are not afraid of hard work. They are willing to put in the effort and sacrifice their time and energy to achieve their goals. They understand that success is not handed to them, but rather earned through discipline and determination.

They stay focused on their goals: Millionaires know what they want and remain focused on achieving it. They don't let distractions or setbacks derail them from their path. They stay committed to their goals and are willing to make sacrifices to reach them.

They practice self-control: Millionaires are disciplined when it comes to their spending habits. They live below their means and practice self-control when it comes to their finances. They are not swayed by short-term gratification and instead make long-term decisions that benefit them in the future.

They cultivate good habits: Millionaires understand the power of good habits and work to cultivate them daily. They know that small, consistent actions lead to big results, and they make sure their habits align with their goals.

They are accountable: Millionaires take responsibility for their actions and hold themselves accountable for their success or failures. They don't blame others for their setbacks but rather learn from them and adjust their strategies accordingly.

Overall, millionaires understand that discipline is key to achieving success. They prioritize their time, work hard, stay focused on their goals, practice self-control, cultivate good habits, and hold themselves accountable. These are some of the secrets of millionaires that many people may not be aware of.

Millionaires focus on their priorities: They have a clear understanding of what they want to achieve and they prioritize their goals accordingly. They don't waste time on activities that don't align with their goals.

Millionaires have a routine: They have a disciplined routine and stick to it. This includes waking up at the same time every day, exercising regularly, and eating healthy meals.

Millionaires are proactive: They take responsibility for their actions and are proactive in achieving their goals. They don't wait for opportunities to come to them; instead, they create their own opportunities.

Millionaires are persistent: They don't give up easily and are willing to put in the hard work and effort required to achieve their goals. They are determined to succeed and won't let setbacks or obstacles deter them.

Millionaires are focused: They have a laser-like focus on their goals and are not distracted by other things. They avoid multitasking and instead concentrate on one task at a time to ensure that it is done to the best of their ability.

Millionaires are self-motivated

They don't rely on external factors to motivate them. Instead, they are self-motivated and driven by their own desire to succeed.

One of the secrets of millionaires that many people don't know about is that they are highly self-motivated. Unlike most people who rely on external motivation to get things done, millionaires have a burning desire within them that propels them forward.

This self-motivation comes from having a clear purpose and passion for what they do. They know what they want to achieve and why they want to achieve it. This clarity gives them the drive and determination to keep going, even when things get tough.

Another secret of self-motivated millionaires is that they have a strong work ethic. They understand that success requires hard work and are willing to put in the effort to achieve their goals. They don't wait for someone else to tell them what to do or push them to get things done. They take responsibility for their own success and are willing to do whatever it takes to make it happen.

Finally, millionaires are masters at self-discipline. They understand that success is not just about what you do, but also about what you don't do. They have the discipline to say no to distractions and time-wasting activities, and the focus to stay on task and complete their work efficiently.

If you want to become a millionaire, developing self-motivation, a strong work ethic, and self-discipline are essential. These qualities will help you stay focused and motivated, even when faced with challenges, and will give you the drive to achieve your goals and create the life you desire.

They have a clear purpose: Millionaires have a clear understanding of what they want to achieve in life, and this purpose drives them to work hard and stay motivated. They have a compelling reason for why they do what they do, and this keeps them focused on their goals.

They set ambitious goals: Millionaires set ambitious goals for themselves and push themselves to achieve them. They are not satisfied with mediocre results, and they constantly strive to improve their performance.

They embrace challenges: Millionaires view challenges as opportunities for growth and development. They are not afraid to step out of their comfort zone and take on new and challenging tasks.

They stay positive: Millionaires have a positive attitude towards life and work. They do not let setbacks or failures bring them down, and they remain optimistic and confident in their abilities.

They surround themselves with positive influences: Millionaires surround themselves with people who inspire and motivate them. They seek out mentors and role models who can help them grow and learn.

They continuously learn and improve: Millionaires are always learning and improving themselves. They read books, attend seminars, and seek out new experiences that can help them grow and develop.

They take action: Millionaires are not afraid to take action and make things happen. They do not wait for opportunities to come to them; they create their own opportunities through hard work and determination.

By adopting these self-motivation strategies, you can develop the mindset of a millionaire and achieve your own success.

Millionaires have self-control: They are disciplined in their spending habits and don't succumb to impulse purchases. They also have the self-control to avoid unhealthy habits like excessive drinking or gambling.

Overall, the key to success is to be disciplined in all areas of your life. This includes your thoughts, actions, and habits. By adopting a disciplined approach, you can achieve your goals and live the life you desire.

Millionaires give back to their communities: Many millionaires are philanthropic and give back to their communities. They recognize that their success is not only due to their own efforts, but also to the support of others. By giving back, they are able to make a positive impact and help others achieve their own success.

Millionaires take action: Successful millionaires take action towards their goals. They do not wait for opportunities to come to them, but instead create their own opportunities through hard work and persistence. By taking action, they are able to achieve their dreams and create the life they desire.

CHAPTER *6*

THE SCIENCE BEHIND AFFIRMATIONS

Affirmations are more than just positive thinking or wishful statements. In fact, there is a science behind affirmations that many people may not be aware of.

The science behind affirmations is rooted in the concept of neuroplasticity, which is the brain's ability to form new neural connections and change existing ones. Essentially, the more you repeat a thought or behavior, the stronger the neural connection becomes. This is why repeated negative thoughts can be harmful, as they can create negative neural pathways in the brain.

On the other hand, affirmations can create positive neural pathways in the brain, leading to increased positivity and confidence. When you repeat positive affirmations, you are strengthening the neural connections associated with those thoughts and beliefs, which can lead to positive changes in behavior and mindset.

Furthermore, affirmations can activate the reticular activating system (RAS) in the brain. The RAS is responsible for filtering sensory information and determining what is important to focus on. When you repeat affirmations, you are essentially telling your brain what is important and what to focus on, which can help you recognize and attract opportunities that align with your affirmations.

So, the science behind affirmations is all about rewiring your brain to think and believe in positive ways, creating new neural connections and activating the RAS to help you achieve your goals. Millionaires understand the power of affirmations and use them regularly to reprogram their mindset for success.

Affirmations are based on the principle of positive thinking, which has been widely studied and proven to have psychological benefits. The human mind is powerful and can be programmed to believe and achieve anything, given the right stimulus. Affirmations are a form of self-talk that can help reprogram the subconscious mind with positive thoughts and beliefs.

Research has shown that affirmations can help reduce stress, improve self-esteem, and increase feelings of well-being. In a study conducted by the University of Pennsylvania, researchers found that affirmations can be an effective tool for managing stress and promoting positive emotions.

When you repeat an affirmation to yourself, your brain starts to create new neural pathways, which can help to change your thought patterns and beliefs. This is because the brain responds to repetition, and the more you repeat a thought or belief, the more it becomes ingrained in your subconscious mind.

Furthermore, affirmations can activate the reward centers in your brain, releasing dopamine, which is a neurotransmitter associated with pleasure and motivation. This can help to reinforce positive thoughts and emotions and make you more motivated to pursue your goals.

Affirmations are based on the science of positive thinking and can help reprogram the subconscious mind with positive thoughts and beliefs. Repeating affirmations can help create new neural pathways, activate reward centers in the brain, and promote feelings of well-being and motivation.

How to create effective affirmations

First, it's important to understand that effective affirmations are positive, present tense statements that are aligned with your goals and values. They should be specific and tailored to your individual needs and desires.

Use positive language: Make sure your affirmations are framed in positive language. Instead of saying "I don't want to be broke anymore," say "I am financially abundant and successful."

Be specific: The more specific you can be with your affirmations, the better. Instead of saying "I want to be successful," say "I am a successful entrepreneur who has built a thriving business."

Use the present tense: Affirmations should be written in the present tense, as if you have already achieved your goal. For example, instead of saying "I will be confident in social situations," say "I am confident and at ease in social situations."

Align with your values: Make sure your affirmations align with your values and beliefs. If you don't truly believe in what you're saying, your affirmations will not be effective.

Repeat them often: Repeat your affirmations often, ideally several times a day. This will help reinforce the positive messages and beliefs you are trying to internalize.

Remember, creating effective affirmations is just one piece of the puzzle when it comes to achieving success. It's important to also adopt a positive mindset, set clear goals, and take consistent action towards your objectives. By combining these strategies, you can create a powerful foundation for achieving your dreams and creating a life of abundance and fulfillment.

Tips for incorporating affirmations into your daily routine

Incorporating affirmations into your daily routine can help you to achieve success in any area of your life. Here are some tips on how to effectively incorporate affirmations into your daily routine, as shared by successful millionaires:

Write your affirmations down: Writing your affirmations down can help you to internalize them and make them more meaningful. Write them down on a piece of paper or in a journal, and read them aloud to yourself every day.

Repeat them often: The more you repeat your affirmations, the more they will become ingrained in your mind. Try repeating them to yourself several times a day, or even setting reminders on your phone or computer to repeat them at certain times.

Use visualization: When you repeat your affirmations, try to visualize yourself achieving the goals you are affirming. Imagine yourself in vivid detail, and feel the emotions associated with achieving those goals.

Use present tense: When creating your affirmations, use the present tense as if you have already achieved your goals. For example, instead of saying "I will be wealthy," say "I am wealthy."

Use positive language: Affirmations should always be stated in a positive way. Focus on what you want to achieve, rather than what you don't want to happen.

By incorporating affirmations into your daily routine in a deliberate and intentional way, you can tap into the power of the mind to achieve your goals and become more successful in all areas of your life.

Repeat your affirmations in the morning: Start your day off on a positive note by repeating your affirmations first thing in the morning. This will set a positive tone for your day and help you stay focused on your goals.

Use visual aids: Create visual aids to accompany your affirmations, such as a vision board or a daily reminder on your phone. These can help keep your affirmations top of mind and reinforce your positive beliefs.

Repeat affirmations during downtime: Incorporate affirmations into your downtime throughout the day, such as during your commute or while waiting in line. This can help you stay focused and motivated.

Believe in your affirmations: It's important to truly believe in the affirmations you are repeating. If you don't believe in what you're saying, it won't be effective. Take the time to choose affirmations that resonate with you and align with your goals and values.

Monitor your progress: Keep track of your progress over time by journaling or taking note of positive changes in your life. This can help you stay motivated and reinforce the power of affirmations in achieving your goals.

PART 5
Overcoming Limiting Beliefs

Chapter 7
Overcoming Limiting Beliefs

Overcoming limiting beliefs is crucial to achieving success in any area of life, and it's a secret that many millionaires have discovered. Our beliefs are powerful, and they can either propel us forward or hold us back. Limiting beliefs are those negative beliefs that we have about ourselves, others, or the world that hold us back from achieving our goals.

One of the secrets of millionaires is that they have mastered the art of identifying and overcoming limiting beliefs. They understand that their beliefs are not necessarily facts, but rather interpretations of their experiences. They know that their beliefs can be changed and that they can choose to adopt empowering beliefs that will help them achieve their goals.

To overcome limiting beliefs, the first step is to identify them. You need to become aware of the negative beliefs that are holding you back. Once you have identified your limiting beliefs, you can start to challenge them. Ask yourself if they are really true or if they are just interpretations of your experiences. Challenge yourself to see things differently and adopt empowering beliefs.

Another secret of millionaires is that they surround themselves with positive influences. They seek out mentors and coaches who can help them identify and overcome their limiting beliefs. They also surround themselves with positive and supportive people who encourage and uplift them.

Visualization and affirmations are also powerful tools that millionaires use to overcome limiting beliefs. By visualizing and affirming positive outcomes, they are able to reprogram their subconscious minds with new empowering beliefs. This helps them to overcome their limiting beliefs and achieve their goals.

Finally, millionaires understand that overcoming limiting beliefs is an ongoing process. They are constantly learning and growing, and they know that there will always be new limiting beliefs to overcome. But they also know that by staying focused and committed to their goals, they can achieve anything they set their minds to.

Recognize and question your limiting beliefs: The first step in overcoming limiting beliefs is to become aware of them. Ask yourself what beliefs might be holding you back in certain areas of your life. Once you have identified a limiting belief, question it. Ask yourself if it's really true or if there's evidence to the contrary.

Reframe your beliefs: Instead of focusing on the negative aspects of your limiting beliefs, reframe them in a positive light. For example, instead of thinking "I'm not good enough," reframe it as "I am capable and have the skills to succeed."

Take action: Often, the best way to overcome limiting beliefs is to take action despite them. When you prove to yourself that you can succeed, it helps to break down those negative beliefs.

Surround yourself with positive influences: Spend time with people who have a positive mindset and encourage you to achieve your goals. Read books and listen to podcasts that inspire and motivate you.

Use visualization and affirmations: Visualization and affirmations can be powerful tools for overcoming limiting beliefs. Visualize yourself achieving your goals and repeat positive affirmations to yourself daily.

Remember, limiting beliefs are just thoughts, and thoughts can be changed. By taking action and using positive tools and influences, you can overcome limiting beliefs and achieve success in all areas of your life.

Identifying and challenging limiting beliefs

Identifying and challenging limiting beliefs is a crucial step in achieving success and wealth. Here are some secrets of millionaires that many people do not know about:

Recognize your limiting beliefs: The first step to overcoming your limiting beliefs is to recognize them. This can be difficult, as these beliefs are often deeply ingrained and subconscious. Pay attention to negative self-talk and areas where you may have self-doubt.

Challenge your beliefs: Once you have identified your limiting beliefs, challenge them. Ask yourself if they are really true, and look for evidence to the contrary. This can help you see things from a different perspective and break free from your limiting beliefs.

Reframe your beliefs: Reframing your beliefs can be a powerful way to overcome them. Instead of seeing a situation as a failure, for example, see it as a learning opportunity. This can help you adopt a growth mindset and see challenges as opportunities for growth.

Take action: Finally, take action to overcome your limiting beliefs. This might involve practicing positive self-talk, seeking out mentors or coaches, or taking steps outside of your comfort zone. The more you challenge your beliefs and take action, the more you will be able to break free from your limitations and achieve success.

Remember, limiting beliefs are just that – beliefs. They are not necessarily based in reality, and they can be changed. By identifying, challenging, and reframing your limiting beliefs, you can unlock your full potential and achieve the success and wealth that you desire.

Seek out evidence to support your new beliefs: One effective way to challenge your limiting beliefs is to seek out evidence that supports a new, more positive belief. For example, if you have a limiting belief that you're not good enough to succeed, you could look for examples of people who started out in a similar position to you and have gone on to achieve great things.

Surround yourself with positive influences: The people you surround yourself with can have a big impact on your beliefs and mindset. Seek out positive, supportive people who believe in you and your potential, and spend less time around those who bring you down or reinforce negative beliefs.

Practice visualization: Visualization can be a powerful tool for challenging limiting beliefs. Take some time each day to visualize yourself achieving your goals, and focus on how it would feel to have your limiting beliefs proven wrong.

Use affirmations: Affirmations can also be helpful in challenging limiting beliefs. Create affirmations that counteract your limiting beliefs and repeat them to yourself regularly, until they start to become a natural part of your thought process.

Focus on progress, not perfection: Finally, it's important to remember that overcoming limiting beliefs is a process, and it won't happen overnight. Don't beat yourself up if you slip back into old patterns of thinking from time to time. Instead, focus on making progress and taking small steps toward your goals each day. With time and practice, you can overcome your limiting beliefs and achieve the success you desire.

Techniques for replacing limiting beliefs with positive ones

I'd be happy to share some techniques for replacing limiting beliefs with positive ones, as part of my advice on the secrets of millionaires that many people do not know about.

Reframe limiting beliefs: One technique for replacing limiting beliefs is to reframe them in a more positive and empowering way. For example, instead of thinking "I'm not good enough," reframe it as "I'm constantly improving and learning."

Practice positive self-talk

Another technique is to practice positive self-talk by speaking to yourself in an empowering and supportive way. Use positive affirmations and remind yourself of your strengths and accomplishments.

Positive self-talk is an essential tool that millionaires use to maintain a positive mindset and overcome challenges. It involves using affirming and encouraging language when speaking to oneself. The secret behind positive self-talk is that it can help to rewire your brain and create new positive thought patterns.

Many people underestimate the power of their own words and thoughts. They may engage in negative self-talk without even realizing it, which can undermine their confidence and limit their potential for success. Millionaires understand that their thoughts and words have a direct impact on their actions and outcomes, so they make a conscious effort to practice positive self-talk.

To practice positive self-talk, start by becoming aware of your thoughts and words. When you notice a negative thought or self-criticism, challenge it and replace it with a positive affirmation. For example, instead of saying "I can't do this," say "I am capable of handling this challenge."

Another helpful technique is to visualize yourself succeeding and achieving your goals. Use positive and affirming language when describing this visualization. For example, "I am confident, strong, and successful."

Incorporating positive self-talk into your daily routine takes practice, but the benefits are worth it. With time and consistency, you can rewire your brain to think positively and overcome limiting beliefs, leading to greater success and fulfillment in life.

Visualize success: Visualization can help to replace limiting beliefs by creating a mental picture of success and achievement. Visualize yourself achieving your goals and breaking through any obstacles.

Surround yourself with positivity: Surrounding yourself with positive people, messages, and experiences can help to reinforce positive beliefs and counteract limiting beliefs. Seek out supportive relationships and positive environments.

Take action: Finally, taking action towards your goals can help to replace limiting beliefs with positive ones. By taking steps towards your goals, you build evidence of your abilities and reinforce positive beliefs about yourself.

These are just a few techniques that can be helpful in replacing limiting beliefs with positive ones. Remember that it takes time and effort to overcome limiting beliefs, but with persistence and determination, anyone can do it.

Visualization: Visualize yourself as already having achieved the success you desire. Create a vivid mental image of yourself in that reality, and really feel the emotions associated with it. This will help to reprogram your subconscious mind to accept the new positive belief.

Positive Affirmations: Create positive affirmations that counteract your limiting belief. Repeat them to yourself every day, and make them a part of your daily routine.

Evidence Gathering: Gather evidence that contradicts your limiting belief. This can be achieved by researching the success stories of people who have overcome similar challenges, and reminding yourself of your own past successes.

Cognitive Behavioral Therapy (CBT): This is a form of talk therapy that helps you to identify and change negative thought patterns. It can be an effective tool for replacing limiting beliefs with positive ones.

Gratitude Journaling: Start a gratitude journal and write down things you are grateful for every day. This can help shift your focus from negative beliefs to positive ones, and help you to appreciate the abundance in your life.

By implementing these techniques, you can begin to replace limiting beliefs with positive ones, and start living the life you truly desire.

How to maintain a positive mindset

Maintaining a positive mindset is crucial for achieving success in any area of life. Here are some tips to help you maintain a positive mindset:

Surround yourself with positive people: The people you surround yourself with can have a huge impact on your mindset. Surround yourself with positive, supportive people who encourage you to be your best self.

Focus on the present moment: Dwelling on the past or worrying about the future can lead to negative thoughts and emotions. Focus on the present moment and what you can do right now to move forward.

Practice gratitude: Practicing gratitude is a powerful way to maintain a positive mindset. Take time each day to reflect on the things you're grateful for, no matter how small they may seem.

Use positive affirmations: Use positive affirmations to reprogram your subconscious mind and cultivate a positive mindset. Repeat positive affirmations to yourself regularly, such as "I am worthy of success" or "I am capable of achieving my goals."

Engage in positive activities: Engage in activities that bring you joy and positivity, such as exercise, meditation, or spending time with loved ones.

Learn from challenges: Challenges and setbacks are a natural part of life, but they can also be opportunities for growth and learning. Instead of dwelling on the negative aspects of a challenge, focus on what you can learn from it and how you can use that knowledge to grow and improve.

By incorporating these practices into your daily life, you can maintain a positive mindset that will help you achieve your goals and create the life you desire.

Practice gratitude: Cultivate a habit of focusing on the good things in your life and expressing gratitude for them. This can be as simple as making a list of things you're grateful for each day or taking time to appreciate the small moments in life.

Surround yourself with positivity: Seek out people and environments that are positive and uplifting. Spend time with people who inspire you and avoid those who bring you down.

Practice mindfulness: Being present in the moment and aware of your thoughts and feelings can help you stay centered and calm, even in challenging situations. Incorporate mindfulness practices, such as meditation or deep breathing, into your daily routine.

Reframe negative thoughts: When negative thoughts arise, consciously work to reframe them in a more positive light. Instead of dwelling on what's going wrong, focus on what you can do to improve the situation.

Stay committed to your goals: Having a clear sense of purpose and direction can help you stay motivated and positive. Set clear goals for yourself and stay committed to achieving them, even when faced with obstacles or setbacks.

Remember, maintaining a positive mindset is a daily practice, but the more you work at it, the more natural it will become.

PART 6
Habits of Successful Passive Income Earners

CHAPTER *8*

HABITS OF SUCCESSFUL PASSIVE INCOME EARNERS

I can tell you that many millionaires have achieved their wealth through passive income streams. Here are some habits of successful passive income earners:

Invest in income-producing assets: Successful passive income earners invest their money in assets that generate income, such as rental properties, dividend-paying stocks, and royalty-generating intellectual property.

Diversify their income streams: They don't rely on a single source of passive income, but instead have multiple income streams to ensure that they are not reliant on any one source of income.

Continuously educate themselves: They stay informed about new investment opportunities and trends in the market to identify new potential income streams.

Automate their income: They set up systems to automate the process of generating passive income, such as hiring property managers or using automatic investment tools.

Live below their means: Successful passive income earners are disciplined in their spending habits and prioritize saving and investing a portion of their income.

Network with other successful investors: They surround themselves with like-minded individuals who can share knowledge and experience to help them grow their wealth.

Set clear financial goals: They have a specific financial goal in mind, and they work hard to achieve it. They monitor their progress and make adjustments as needed to ensure they stay on track.

These are just a few habits of successful passive income earners. Remember, achieving financial success through passive income requires dedication, discipline, and a willingness to continuously learn and adapt.

Continuously educate themselves: Successful passive income earners understand the importance of staying informed about their industry and the latest trends. They read books, attend seminars, and participate in online courses to expand their knowledge.

Automate their income streams: Passive income earners automate their income streams by using tools such as autoresponders and payment processors. This allows them to earn money even while they sleep.

Diversify their income streams: They understand the importance of diversifying their income streams to reduce risk and increase their chances of success. They have multiple sources of passive income that complement each other.

Invest in marketing: Passive income earners invest in marketing to promote their products and reach a wider audience. They use various marketing channels such as social media, email marketing, and paid advertising.

Focus on providing value: They focus on providing value to their customers by creating high-quality products and services that solve their problems. They prioritize customer satisfaction and aim to exceed their expectations.

Manage their time effectively: Passive income earners understand the importance of managing their time effectively. They prioritize their tasks and delegate when necessary to focus on income-generating activities.

Embrace failure: They understand that failure is part of the process and view it as an opportunity to learn and grow. They use failures as feedback to improve their products and services.

I hope these additional habits provide you with some valuable insights into the secrets of successful passive income earners.

The habits that lead to financial success

here are some habits that millionaires practice that lead to financial success:

Setting clear financial goals: Millionaires set specific, measurable, achievable, relevant, and time-bound financial goals. They regularly review their progress towards these goals and adjust their plans accordingly.

Living below their means: Millionaires are frugal and live below their means. They spend less than they earn and save or invest the difference.

Prioritizing savings and investments: Millionaires prioritize saving and investing their money for the long-term. They know that small savings and investments can compound over time and lead to significant wealth.

Developing multiple streams of income: Millionaires often have multiple streams of income. They diversify their income sources to protect themselves from economic downturns and to maximize their earning potential.

Educating themselves about money: Millionaires are always learning about personal finance, investing, and entrepreneurship. They read books, attend seminars, and seek out mentors to improve their financial knowledge and skills.

Taking calculated risks: Millionaires are not afraid to take calculated risks. They understand that there are risks involved in investing and entrepreneurship, but they weigh the potential rewards against the risks before making a decision.

Being persistent and resilient: Millionaires know that success does not happen overnight. They are persistent and resilient, and they don't give up when faced with setbacks or failures. They learn from their mistakes and keep moving forward towards their goals.

Overall, these habits require discipline, hard work, and a willingness to take risks. By adopting these habits, anyone can increase their chances of achieving financial success.

As a millionaire and success coach, I can tell you that one of the biggest secrets to financial success is to develop and maintain good habits. Here are some habits that have helped many successful people to achieve their financial goals:

Live below your means: Millionaires understand the importance of saving and investing, and one way to do that is to spend less than you earn. This means being mindful of your expenses and avoiding unnecessary purchases.

Budgeting: Creating a budget helps you track your income and expenses and ensures that you're living within your means. It's important to prioritize saving and investing in your budget.

Continuous learning: Successful people never stop learning. They invest in their education and skills to stay relevant and competitive in their industry.

Networking: Building a strong network of like-minded individuals is important for personal and professional growth. You can learn from others' experiences and gain new opportunities by connecting with others.

Goal-setting: Setting specific, measurable, achievable, relevant, and time-bound (SMART) goals helps you stay focused and motivated. It's important to have both short-term and long-term goals.

Persistence: Building wealth takes time, and there will be setbacks and failures along the way. Successful people understand the importance of persistence and perseverance in achieving their goals.

Giving back: Many successful people also prioritize giving back to their communities and those in need. Giving back not only benefits others, but it also brings personal fulfillment and satisfaction.

These habits are not limited to financial success but can also be applied to other areas of life. Remember, developing good habits takes time and effort, but the rewards can be life-changing.

How to develop successful habits

Developing successful habits is an essential part of achieving financial success. Here are some tips on how to develop successful habits:

Set clear goals: Before you start working on developing new habits, you need to have a clear idea of what you want to achieve. Set specific, measurable goals and make sure they align with your values and priorities.

Start small: Don't try to change everything at once. Instead, focus on developing one or two new habits at a time. Start with something small and manageable, and build up from there.

Create a plan: Develop a plan for how you will implement your new habits. Decide when and where you will perform them, and create a schedule to help you stay on track.

Track your progress: Keep track of your progress as you work on developing new habits. This will help you stay motivated and identify areas where you need to improve.

Stay committed: Developing new habits takes time and effort, so it's important to stay committed to your goals. Don't let setbacks or obstacles discourage you. Keep pushing forward, and stay focused on your long-term objectives.

Remember, developing successful habits is not a one-time event, but an ongoing process. By setting clear goals, starting small, creating a plan, tracking your progress, and staying committed, you can develop the habits that will help you achieve financial success.

Tips for maintaining successful habits long-term

Stay committed: Success is a journey, not a destination. It requires daily commitment and consistency. Make your goals a top priority and keep them in mind every day.

Create a routine: Successful people often have daily routines that help them stay on track. Identify the habits that are most important to you and create a routine that incorporates them.

Stay focused: Avoid distractions and stay focused on your goals. Learn to say no to things that are not aligned with your priorities.

Measure progress: Regularly measure your progress towards your goals. Celebrate your successes and learn from your failures.

Hold yourself accountable: Take responsibility for your actions and hold yourself accountable. Don't make excuses or blame others for your shortcomings.

Surround yourself with positive influences: Surround yourself with people who support and encourage you. Avoid negative influences that may discourage or distract you from your goals.

Stay motivated: Keep your goals in mind and stay motivated. Remind yourself why you started and visualize the rewards of your success.

Remember, success is not achieved overnight. It requires daily effort and commitment. By following these tips, you can develop and maintain successful habits that will lead you to long-term success.

Part 7
Mastering Your Mindset

CHAPTER *9*

MASTERING YOUR MINDSET

Mastering your mindset is a crucial step in achieving financial success. Your thoughts and beliefs have a profound impact on your actions and the results you achieve in life. Here are some secrets of millionaires that many people may not know about when it comes to mastering your mindset:

Focus on abundance: Millionaires have a mindset of abundance, believing that there are unlimited opportunities and resources available to them. They focus on what they have, rather than what they lack, and are grateful for what they receive.

As a wealth coach, I can tell you that focusing on abundance is a key mindset that successful people have. When you focus on abundance, you are training your mind to see opportunities and possibilities rather than limitations and scarcity. This is because your mindset creates your reality, and if you believe that abundance is available to you, you will start to see opportunities to create it.

They believe that there is enough to go around. Many people have a scarcity mindset, where they believe that there is a limited amount of money or success to be had, and that if someone else is successful, it means there is less for them. Millionaires, on the other hand, believe that there is enough success to go around, and that everyone can be successful if they are willing to put in the work.

They focus on what they can give, not just what they can get. Millionaires understand that giving back and contributing to others is a key part of abundance. When you give freely, you create positive energy and attract more abundance into your life.

They focus on creating value for others. Rather than just trying to make money, millionaires focus on creating value for others. By creating something that helps others, they are able to attract abundance into their lives.

They practice gratitude. Millionaires understand that being grateful for what they have is a key part of abundance. When you are grateful for what you have, you attract more positive energy and abundance into your life.

They visualize abundance. Millionaires use visualization techniques to help them focus on abundance. By picturing themselves living a life of abundance, they are able to attract more of it into their lives.

Remember, your mindset creates your reality. If you focus on abundance, you will attract more of it into your life.

Believe in yourself: Millionaires have an unshakeable belief in their abilities and their vision for their lives. They don't let setbacks or failures discourage them, but rather see them as opportunities to learn and grow.

Believing in yourself is a crucial factor in achieving success, and it's a common trait among millionaires. One of the secrets of millionaires that many people don't know about is that they have an unshakeable belief in themselves and their abilities.

To believe in yourself, you need to develop a strong sense of self-worth and self-esteem. You must believe that you are capable of achieving great things and that you deserve success. This belief will give you the confidence to pursue your goals and overcome any obstacles that come your way.

Another secret of millionaires is that they focus on their strengths and work to develop them further. Instead of dwelling on their weaknesses or failures, they use their strengths to their advantage and find ways to improve themselves continually. They also surround themselves with positive influences and avoid negative people who may bring them down.

It's important to remember that believing in yourself doesn't mean you'll never fail or make mistakes. It means that you trust yourself to learn from those experiences and continue moving forward towards your goals. This mindset is what sets millionaires apart from those who never achieve their dreams.

To cultivate a strong belief in yourself, start by acknowledging your strengths and accomplishments. Make a list of your achievements and the things you're proud of, no matter how small they may seem. Use these positive experiences to build your confidence and motivate you to take on bigger challenges.

You can also practice positive self-talk and visualization to reinforce your belief in yourself. Instead of dwelling on negative thoughts or self-doubt, focus on positive affirmations and visualize yourself succeeding in your goals.

Remember, the key to believing in yourself is to focus on your strengths, surround yourself with positive influences, and continually work towards improving yourself. With a strong sense of self-worth and belief in your abilities, you can achieve anything you set your mind to.

Develop a growth mindset: Millionaires understand that their abilities and skills can be developed through hard work and dedication. They see challenges as opportunities to stretch themselves and develop new skills.

Visualize success: Millionaires use visualization techniques to see themselves achieving their goals and living their dreams. They create a clear mental picture of what they want to achieve and use this to motivate and inspire them.

Take action: Millionaires understand that mindset alone is not enough – action is required to turn dreams into reality. They take consistent action towards their goals, even if it means stepping out of their comfort zone.

Embrace failure: Millionaires see failure as a necessary part of the learning process. They understand that failure is simply feedback and use it to make adjustments and move forward.

Surround yourself with positivity: Millionaires understand that their environment can have a big impact on their mindset. They surround themselves with positive people who support and encourage them, and limit their exposure to negativity and criticism.

By mastering your mindset and adopting these habits, you can unlock your full potential and achieve financial success. Remember, your thoughts become your reality, so it's important to focus on positivity, abundance, and growth.

Here are some additional secrets of millionaires that many people may not know about in relation to mastering their mindset:

Millionaires practice gratitude: They focus on what they have rather than what they lack, and express gratitude for the blessings in their lives. This positive mindset helps them attract more abundance and success.

Millionaires embrace failure: They understand that failure is a natural part of the learning process and view it as an opportunity to grow and improve. They don't let setbacks or mistakes discourage them, but instead use them as motivation to do better.

Millionaires prioritize their mental and emotional health: They understand the importance of taking care of themselves and their mindset. They engage in practices like meditation, mindfulness, and therapy to manage stress and maintain a positive outlook.

Millionaires surround themselves with positive influences: They understand the impact of the people they spend time with on their mindset and success. They surround themselves with supportive, positive people who uplift and inspire them.

Millionaires set clear goals and intentions: They have a clear vision of what they want to achieve and regularly set goals and intentions to help them get there. This helps them stay focused and motivated, and gives them a sense of purpose and direction.

By mastering their mindset, millionaires are able to overcome obstacles, stay motivated, and achieve their goals. These practices may seem small, but they can have a big impact on success and happiness.

Putting it all together

Putting it all together and achieving financial success is not an overnight process, but rather a journey that requires consistency, hard work, and discipline. Here are some secrets of millionaires that many people do not know about:

Have a clear vision: Millionaires have a clear vision of what they want to achieve and the life they want to live. They know what they want, and they create a plan to achieve it.

Take action: Millionaires take action on their goals and plans. They don't wait for the perfect moment or the perfect opportunity; they take action and adjust their plans as they go.

Develop a positive mindset: Millionaires have a positive mindset that enables them to focus on the opportunities rather than the obstacles. They have faith in themselves and their ability to achieve their goals.

Practice discipline: Millionaires practice discipline in all aspects of their lives. They are disciplined in their spending, their habits, their time management, and their goal setting.

Learn from failures: Millionaires view failures as learning experiences and use them as opportunities to grow and improve. They do not let failures define them or hold them back.

Surround themselves with like-minded individuals: Millionaires surround themselves with other successful and like-minded individuals who share their vision and support their goals.

Continuously educate themselves: Millionaires understand that knowledge is power and continuously educate themselves on their industry, market trends, and personal development.

By incorporating these habits and mindset shifts into your daily routine, you can start to see a positive impact on your financial success. Remember that it takes time and consistency, but with the right mindset and habits, anyone can achieve their financial goals and live the life they desire.

Take action: All the knowledge and motivation in the world won't do you any good if you don't take action. Successful people are not afraid to take risks and try new things. They understand that failure is simply a stepping stone to success and are willing to learn from their mistakes.

Surround yourself with success: Success is contagious, and it's important to surround yourself with people who have a positive mindset and are working towards their own goals. Find a mentor or join a mastermind group to help you stay focused and motivated.

Stay focused on your goals: It's easy to get distracted by the day-to-day tasks and lose sight of your long-term goals. Successful people stay focused on their goals and work diligently towards achieving them, even when it's not easy.

Continuously learn and grow: Successful people never stop learning and growing. They read books, attend seminars, and surround themselves with people who challenge them to be their best. Continuously improving yourself and your skills is essential to achieving long-term success.

Be grateful: Gratitude is an essential component of a successful mindset. Successful people understand that they have been given opportunities that many others have not, and they are grateful for the blessings in their lives. Cultivate a mindset of gratitude and abundance, and you will attract more success into your life.

Remember, success is not just about what you do, but also about who you are. Focus on developing the habits and mindset of successful people, and success will naturally follow.

How to maintain a millionaire mindset long-term

Maintaining a millionaire mindset long-term requires ongoing commitment and effort, but it is possible with the right mindset and habits. Here are some tips on how to maintain a millionaire mindset long-term:

Surround yourself with positive influences: The people you surround yourself with can have a significant impact on your mindset. Surround yourself with people who are supportive, positive, and have a similar mindset to you.

Continuously learn and grow: Millionaires never stop learning and growing. They are always seeking out new knowledge, skills, and experiences to help them improve and achieve their goals.

Keep a positive attitude: A positive attitude is essential to maintaining a millionaire mindset. Instead of focusing on problems and setbacks, focus on solutions and opportunities.

Stay focused on your goals: Millionaires are laser-focused on their goals and take action to achieve them. Stay focused on your goals and take consistent action towards achieving them.

Embrace failure: Failure is a natural part of the journey towards success. Embrace failure as an opportunity to learn and grow, rather than something to fear or avoid.

Practice gratitude: Millionaires understand the power of gratitude and make it a daily habit. Practicing gratitude helps you stay focused on what you have rather than what you lack.

Develop a positive self-image: Your self-image is how you see yourself, and it can impact your mindset and actions. Develop a positive self-image by focusing on your strengths, accomplishments, and potential.

Remember, maintaining a millionaire mindset long-term is not a one-time event, but rather an ongoing process. It requires dedication, commitment, and effort, but the rewards are well worth it.

Surround yourself with like-minded people: It's important to surround yourself with people who share your goals and mindset. This will help you stay motivated and focused on your goals.

Continuously learn and grow: Successful people never stop learning. Make a habit of reading books, attending seminars, and networking with successful people to stay up-to-date with the latest trends and best practices in your industry.

Take action: A millionaire mindset is not just about thinking positively; it's also about taking action. Make a plan, set goals, and take consistent action towards achieving them.

Embrace failure: Failure is a part of the journey towards success. Instead of letting failures get you down, use them as an opportunity to learn and grow.

Practice gratitude: Focusing on what you have rather than what you lack is key to maintaining a positive mindset. Take time each day to reflect on the things you are grateful for.

Remember, maintaining a millionaire mindset is an ongoing process. It takes consistent effort and a commitment to personal growth and development.

Strategies for continuing personal growth and success

Continuing personal growth and success are essential for maintaining a millionaire mindset long-term. Here are some strategies that successful millionaires use to continue their personal growth and success:

Invest in education: Successful millionaires never stop learning. They invest in their education through books, courses, seminars, and conferences. By continuously learning and expanding their knowledge, they stay ahead of the game and can apply new skills and ideas to their businesses.

Seek out mentors: Having a mentor can provide valuable insights, advice, and guidance. Successful millionaires seek out mentors who have achieved the level of success they desire and learn from their experiences.

Embrace challenges: Successful millionaires understand that challenges are opportunities for growth. Instead of avoiding challenges, they embrace them and use them as opportunities to learn and improve.

Surround themselves with successful people: Surrounding themselves with successful people provides inspiration, motivation, and support. Successful millionaires build relationships with other successful people who share their goals and values.

Take calculated risks: Successful millionaires are not afraid to take risks. However, they do not take reckless risks. They evaluate risks carefully and take calculated risks that have the potential for high rewards.

Stay focused on their goals: Successful millionaires stay focused on their goals and maintain a clear vision of what they want to achieve. They set specific, measurable goals and create plans to achieve them.

Practice gratitude: Successful millionaires appreciate what they have and practice gratitude for their success. Gratitude helps them stay positive and motivated, even during challenging times.

By implementing these strategies, successful millionaires continue to grow personally and professionally and maintain their millionaire mindset long-term.

Always be learning: Successful people never stop learning. They understand the importance of acquiring new knowledge and skills to keep up with a changing world. Make a habit of reading books, attending workshops, and taking courses to expand your knowledge.

Surround yourself with positive people: Your social circle can have a significant impact on your mindset and motivation.

Surround yourself with people who uplift and inspire you, and limit your exposure to negative influences.

Stay committed to your goals: Consistency is key to achieving long-term success. Stay committed to your goals, even when the going gets tough. Remember that setbacks and failures are a natural part of the journey, and use them as opportunities to learn and grow.

Continually evaluate and adjust your strategies: The world is constantly changing, and so should your strategies for success. Continually evaluate your methods and adjust your approach as needed to stay relevant and effective.

Practice gratitude: Gratitude is a powerful tool for cultivating a positive mindset. Take time each day to reflect on the things you are grateful for, and express appreciation to the people who have supported you along the way.

Take care of your physical and mental health: Success is not just about wealth and status; it also involves maintaining your physical and mental well-being. Make time for exercise, healthy eating, and self-care practices like meditation and mindfulness.

Remember, success is a journey, not a destination. Continually invest in your personal growth and development, and stay committed to the habits and strategies that have helped you succeed. With persistence and a growth mindset, anything is possible.

www.ingramcontent.com/pod-product-compliance
Lightning Source LLC
Chambersburg PA
CBHW031923240526
45464CB00022B/656